Candace Bahouth's
ROMANTIC NEEDLEPOINT

Love is a canvas pattern furnished by Nature and
embroidered by imagination.

VOLTAIRE (1694–1778)

Candace Bahouth's
Romantic Needlepoint

20 Needlepoint Designs Inspired by Love

Special Photography by Linda Burgess

A Bulfinch Press Book
Little, Brown and Company
Boston New York Toronto London

For
Milly-doo

Love many, trust few,
always paddle your own canoe.

First North American Edition

CHART ILLUSTRATOR Colin Salmon
DIAGRAMS Alison Barratt

ISBN 0-8212-2238-4

Library of Congress Catalog Card Number 95-78652

Bulfinch Press is an imprint and trademark of Little, Brown and Company (Inc.)
Published simultaneously in Canada by Little, Brown & Company (Canada) Limited

PRINTED IN ITALY

CONTENTS

INTRODUCTION

Love is the emotion, the energized thought, I want to convey to you in this book. I want to show you its active power: as a force, a transformer, and an illuminator.

Love is the generator that propels us to make; to create. And the result of this creative love inevitably manifests itself in some tangible form: in children, music, a chair, a cathedral, a garden, a loaf of bread, a friendship —or needlework.

A nd all work is empty save when there is love... and what is it to work with love? It is to weave a cloth with threads drawn from your heart, even as if your beloved were to wear that cloth; it is to build a house with affection, even as if your beloved were to dwell in that house; it is to sow seeds with tenderness and reap the harvest with joy even as if your beloved were to eat the fruit... work is love made visible.

THE PROPHET, KAHLIL GIBRAN (1883–1931)

When I make something with my hands rather than with a machine, I infuse it and enrich it with love. It expresses what I often cannot express in words; it becomes like an unspoken conversation between me and the recipient. Our feelings and thoughts for the other person so permeate us, that they unconsciously go straight from our heart and head down to our fingers and elevate the work. A sense of loss, loyalty, enrapture can become a

A few tokens of love from my own collection of eclectic objects (above and left)

7

*S*ome flowers must be bright with
poetry, some dark and smudged
with war; others vivid and bizarre with
thoughts of life; and a lovely rose will
always speak of the fragile beauty of love
and friendship.

LADY OTTOLINE MORRELL (1873–1938),
ON THE SUBJECT OF HER NEEDLEWORK

How wonderfully alive and at peace the maker feels when "doing" his or her work. Whether it is music, painting, gardening, metal working, or brick laying, the work impassions and animates one's whole being.

William Morris's daughter May wrote: "Homemade needlework should be irresponsible, gay, a little absurd sometimes, and very personal." I like the "very personal." The labor of love that takes patience and care to complete is worthy of the recipient.

Romance can be a very nebulous term, but for me it conjures up a certain atmosphere: one of voluptuous flowers, fantasy, imagination, exoticism, colors that tickle the eye, nonsense, and tenderness. A romantic picture or a poem tends to inspire a rush of emotions —throwing the recipient into a panoply of creative, lustful, dreamy, and elated thoughts.

parcel of meanings, of things meant, or even "a talisman of fecundity." Blaise Pascal wrote: "The heart has its reasons, which reason knows nothing of."

As well as being stimulated and nourished, the maker is given gifts not so obvious at first —a time for him or herself, a time for imagination, contemplation, and quiet, a time full of absorption and rhythm.

A wonderful example of a "romantic" image is the confident graceful young Pict shown opposite, who has "dressed" herself in a lush excess of flowers. Her long wavy tresses flow out in a wild abandon so typical of many other romantic images that I have chosen to illustrate my book.

In the following chapters I demonstrate how both romance and love, and their effects, have inspired artists and makers for thousands of years. I have, of necessity, simplified and condensed huge areas of thought and experience. Please forgive any generalizations or over-solidifying of anything as complicated and as fluid in its nature as love.

When you work, let your mood be one, not of indifference, but of zest and zeal. Forget that you may fail; dance between control and abandonment, and learn to trust. Love is not to be trifled with; it is something to be lived to the full.

A selection of some of the old fragments and romantic tokens that inspire my work (below)

♥

Stand up and look at me face to face, friend to friend; unfurl the loveliness in your eyes.

SAPPHO (428–348 BC)

A YOUNG DAUGHTER OF THE PICTS *(left), by Jacques le Moyne de Morgues (c. 1533–1588)*

PAGAN PLEASURES

*T*he wonder and mystery of nature,
with its animals, plants, fish,
seasons, and ever-changing sky, profoundly
influenced pre-Christians. To explain the
inexplicable, they created deities whose
appearance, appetites and actions were
similar to their own but on a nobler scale
—energetic, imaginative, vital,
and creative.

*The Coptic God and Goddess cushion (left), and
a portrait of Dionysus (above), a 5th-century
Coptic textile fragment*

*W*hat delicate stripling is it,
    Pyrrha, that now, steeped
in liquid perfumes, is wooing thee on the
heaped rose-leaves in some pleasant grot?
For whose eyes dost thou braid those
flaxen locks, so trim, so simple?

ODES, HORACE (65–8 BC)

Portrait of a girl with a pen and tablets from Pompeii, 1st-century AD (below), and a fresco from Stabiae, 1st-century AD (right)

*A*t the touch of
    love everyone
becomes a poet.

PLATO (428–348 BC)

All early civilizations worshipped a great mother goddess, a symbol of nature's power and her fruitful forces. This female deity was venerated by different societies in the belief that this would ensure the fertility of crops, as well as of men and women. Gradually, her male consorts took their place beside her on the divine pantheon, and the central myth grew into a complex web of evocative tales. Such stories attempted to rationalize unexplained phenomena and dramatize human behavior. The best fairy tales are rooted in human experience. They represent the eternal in us.

Over time the pre-Christian gods came also to represent inner virtues: imagination, creativity, intellect, moral virtues, and, above all, the ability to love. Deities once associated with the natural world were imbued by the Greeks with their highest aspirations, both intellectual and sensual; and by imitating the gods, they believed they could acquire a god-like power. Aphrodite (Venus to the Romans), responsible for the annual reappearance of spring and the fertility of gardens, became the goddess of love, thus deifying beauty and every act of sensuality. Outward beauty was revered as a reflection of inner perfection in both men and women (expectant mothers would decorate their bedchambers with votive offerings and images of the loveliest of the gods and goddesses), and sexual life was viewed not only as health-giving but as a creative force.

Roman gods were both more eclectic and more utilitarian than those of the Greeks. Specific functions were attributed to them, and religious sacrifices were made to seek favor. The Romans were the first to wear a wedding ring, in the belief that the vein of the third finger led directly to the heart.

Ancient myths inspire us still. We, too, can emulate the gods and be reminded of the god-like nobility that lies within us. We, too, can be inspired and animated as the sap rises in spring, and love and hope are renewed. Images of gods and goddesses speak to us of

*L*ove moves the pure Heaven to wed
    the Earth; and Love takes hold
on Earth to join in marriage. And the
rain, dropping from the husband
Heaven, impregnates Earth, and she
brings forth for men pasture for flocks,
and corn, the life of men.

DANAIDS, AESCHYLUS (5TH CENTURY BC)

the balance between sun and moon, earth and sky, winter and summer, young and old; in the harmonious coupling of male and female forces, a particular kind of beauty is to be found and to be rejoiced in.

EGYPTIAN EYE PURSE

More than five thousand years before Christ, a civilization along the fertile Nile valley produced weaving, glass, jewelry, sculpture, and paintings of a quality that is hard to equal today. The great pyramids at Giza, the colossal statues at Luxor, and the proud sphinxes at Karnak all stand testimony to the importance that gods played in this highly sophisticated culture. In one tomb alone it is reported that over 750 gods are listed in the secret codes of Egyptian hieroglyphics.

O come quickly to your sister
Like a hunted gazelle
bounding across the desert
Its feet falter, its limbs weaken...
May you come to your
beloved's refuge
Kissing her hand four times
You seek the love of your sister...

EGYPTIAN BANQUET SONG, ANON.
(XIX-XX DYNASTY)

The Egyptians worshipped sky, earth, sun, moon, desert, and, above all, animals and the mighty river Nile. The sky was female: Nut, of the starry belly, which men saw shining at night. The earth was male: Geb, lying prone, with his back sprouting all the vegetation of the world.

The alluring eyes, outlined in black, of these two young sisters from an Egyptian tomb (left) were the inspiration for my Egyptian Eye. The snake-tailed or udjat eye was said to be a powerful amulet or magic charm, possessing the power to see all things and to provide universal prosperity. It was the emblem of sovereignty and unlimited power, and was often used in jewelry and mummy wrappings. The left eye represented the moon, the right eye the sun.

I have always loved the elaborate border of this wall painting, and have used it here. I love, too, the gentleness with which one young girl delicately strokes the other's face.

It is true there is always color where the sun shines, and to capture the potency of this talisman I have used the blue of lapis lazuli, the green of powdered malachite, an iron red, which the Egyptians saw as the color of life, and black, the ancient color of fertility, damp caves, and rich soil. By adding some earth-colored beads, I hope I have caught some of the exoticism of this remarkable period.

The Egyptian Eye purse (right), and an Egyptian tomb painting of two sisters (below), dated around 1375–1358 BC, and now in the Ashmolean Museum, Oxford

MAKING THE PURSE

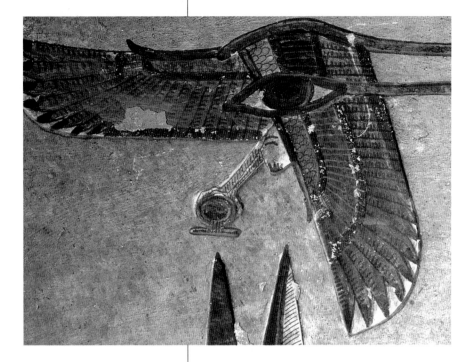

An Egyptian eye detail (above), from the Tomb of Ramses III, at Luxor, Egypt

the various tent-stitch techniques and page 118 for blocking instructions.

One length of cord is used to form the edging and the purse strap. After blocking, line and back the purse (see page 122). Insert one cord end into the small gap left at the top of one seam. Stitch the cord in place along the top, then along the remaining three edges of the needlepoint. Adjust the remaining cord to the desired strap length, then insert the end into the gap on the opposite side of the purse and secure. Add the beaded fringe last.

COLOR KEY

This design was made in Appleton (Ap) tapestry yarn. Alternative yarns listed on page 124 will give a slightly different effect.

MATERIALS

• Appleton tapestry yarn in 8 colors and Twilley's *Goldfingering* (metallic thread) in gold
• 10-mesh ecru double-thread canvas 13 x 13in (33 x 33cm)
• Size 18 tapestry needle
• Small piece of fabric for back of purse and for lining, and matching sewing thread
• 2¼yd (2m) of ready-made gold cord for edging and purse strap
• Assorted beads and strong thread for fringe
Design size: 7 x 7in (18 x 18cm)

WORKING THE DESIGN

The chart is 70 stitches wide and 70 stitches high. Using a single strand of tapestry yarn, or two strands of gold metallic thread, work the design in tent stitch. The color key gives the main uses of each color. See page 116 for

Ap 722 – terracotta – 1 skein
background and lower border pattern

Ap 694 – golden yellow – 1 skein
lower border pattern

Ap 831 – jade green – 1 skein
outer border and lowest border panel

Ap 825 – dark blue – 1 skein
eye and border patterns

Ap 822 – light blue – 1 skein
eye and border patterns

Ap 767 – dark cinnamon – 1 skein
background veins and lower border

Ap 993 – black – 1 skein
eye details

Ap 991 – white – 1 skein
eye details

gold metallic thread – 1 ball
eye outlines and outer border

GREEK URN

Myths in the world of Ancient Greece provided examples of the power of the gods and the noble acts of man; allegory and symbolism helped to explain the unseen forces that drew things together or split them asunder. Eros, God of Love, and son of Zeus and Aphrodite, represented the forces of attraction in bringing "harmony to chaos." He was worshipped as the spiritual form of love, whereas his mother, Aphrodite, was repre-

Do you desire to be wholly one; always day and night in one another's company? for if that is what you desire, I am ready to melt and fuse you together… There is not a man of them who when he heard the proposal would deny or would not acknowledge that this meeting and melting into one another, this becoming one instead of two, was the very expression of his ancient need.

THE SYMPOSIUM, PLATO (424–348 BC)

sentative of sexual love, and thus deemed responsible for the physical passion of man.

Sexual love was spoken of freely, and many of the myths celebrate the co-joining of the deities with humans. Zeus, king of the Gods, was represented as a playboy god, often straying away from Hera, his queen, to enjoy the tempting flesh of mortals. To seduce Leda, he took the form of a swan, and when Europa refused his advances, he disguised himself as a white bull and then carried her away on his back across the water.

Greek imagery is prolific on their black and terracotta painted pottery and reflects the Greek preoccupations of love and life. Cavorting couples burst with vitality, exuberance, and an innocent playfulness that fills me with delight. The word "orgy" comes from the Greek for "night festival," and many a Greek vase tell its tale of wild abandon, passion, love, and bacchanalian reveling.

The inspiration for my shaped cushion was a 6th-century Greek vase, probably representing a marriage or engagement. It shows a fully clothed couple, embracing with tenderness and affection. The formal way they are positioned, in isolation, helps to emphasize the concentration with which they gaze into each other's eyes.

In the spirit of Greek ceramics, I decided to use three simple and dramatic colors—principally black and terracotta, with touches of cream for highlighting the woman's skin. The design could be set within a cream panel or left as a shaped vase. I have added typically Greek motifs: stylized vine leaves, which resemble hearts; and swirls, which represent life's energy, leading us in and out of the labyrinth of existence. Since earliest times man has understood the maze of love; Sophocles said: "One word frees us of all the weight and the pain of life, and that word is Love."

The Greek Urn (left), and the original source (above), a late 6th-century vase

MAKING THE CUSHION

MATERIALS

- Appleton tapestry yarn in 3 colors
- 10-mesh ecru double-thread canvas 21 x 23in (53 x 57cm)
- Size 18 tapestry needle
- ½yd (50cm) of fabric for backing and matching sewing thread
- 13in (33cm) zipper (optional)
- 2yd (1.8m) of black ready-made cord for edging around the shaped cushion
- Pillow form slightly larger than finished needlepoint

Design size: 15 x 16½ in (38 x 42cm)

Persephone and Hades (below), depicted on a 5th-century Greek vase from Vulci

WORKING THE DESIGN

The chart is 150 stitches across the widest point and 165 stitches across the longest point. Mount the canvas on an embroidery frame to ensure that it will retain its shape during stitching. Using a single strand of tapestry yarn, work the design in tent stitch. The color key gives the main uses of each color. See page 116 for tent-stitch techniques and page 118 for blocking instructions.

The blocked needlepoint serves as the template for the fabric backing and as a template for making the shaped pillow form. Detailed instructions for backing shaped cushions are given on page 119.

COLOR KEY

This design was made in Appleton (Ap) tapestry yarn. Alternative yarns listed on page 124 will give a slightly different effect.

Ap 478 – terracotta – 9 skeins
urn patterns
Ap 693 – light golden yellow – 1 skein
woman's face, arm, and feet only
Ap 993 – black – 18 skeins
background and urn patterns

Odysseus and Penelope, after their love had taken its sweet course, turned to the fresh delights of talk.

ODYSSEY, BOOK XXIII, HOMER (C. 900 BC)

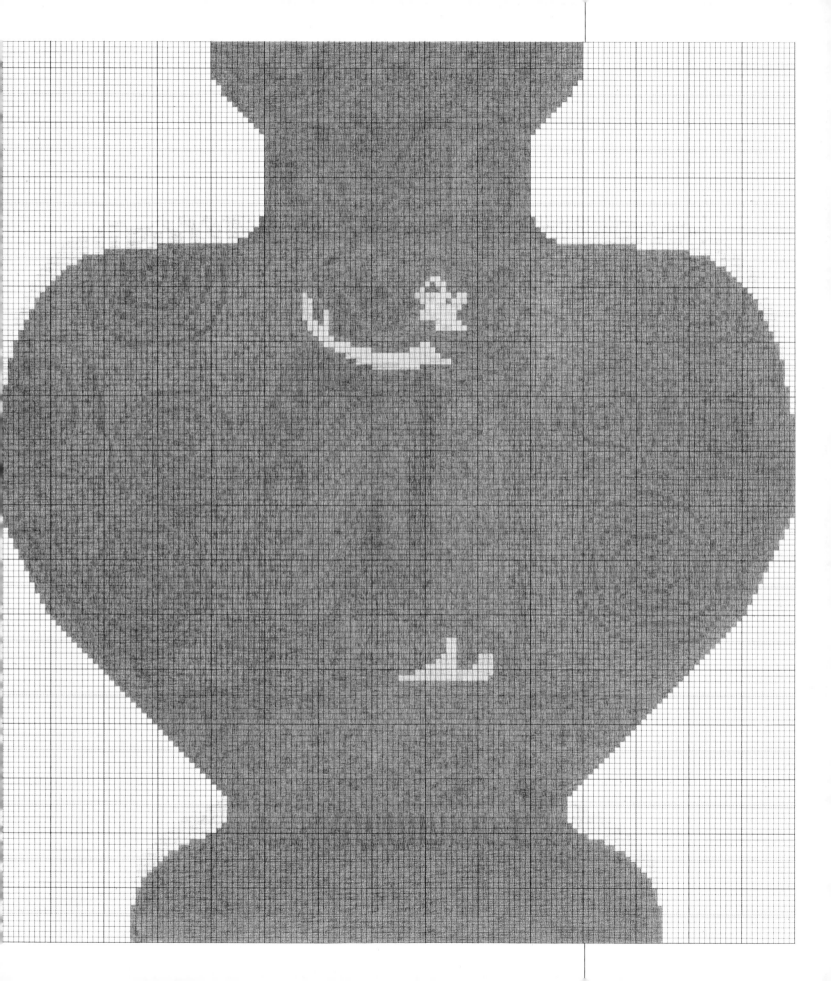

ROMAN HEAD

The 1st-century BC Villa of the Mysteries at Pompeii was the original inspiration for my Roman extravaganza. The frescoes in the villa are believed to illustrate mythological tales of gods and goddesses, and depict the love of Venus and Adonis as well as celebrations of the god Bacchus. The figures are framed against remarkable architectural decoration and detail, as if they were on a stage.

She said no more and as she turned away there was a bright glimpse of the rosy glow of her neck, and from her ambrosial head of hair a heavenly fragrance wafted; her dress flowed down right to her feet, and in her walk it showed, and she was in truth a goddess.

THE AENEID, I, 402, VIRGIL (70–19 BC)

The Roman palette is, to my mind, unsurpassed: the vibrant red, the aubergine vertical stripes edged with gold and verdigris. I have added a sumptuous border of marble to complement the Greek key pattern.

The artist of the handsome female head I finally chose for my work used an encaustic technique, in which the pigment was mixed with hot wax and then applied with a spatula onto wood. Imagine achieving such mastery with such a bizarre technique!

The head probably dates from the time of Nero (see page 24). I love her deep-set, expressive eyes, full of mystery and serenity. The black mass of her hair is highlighted by her jewelry and a wreath of thin gold leaves.

The Roman Head cushion (left), which was inspired by this detail (below), from the Villa dei Misteri, Pompeii

MAKING THE CUSHION

The 1st-century Roman portrait (above), which was the source for the needlepoint

*B*ut what a woman says to her lusting lover it is best to write in wind and swift-flowing water.

CATALLUS (87–54 BC)

MATERIALS
• Appleton tapestry yarn in 17 colors
• 10-mesh ecru double-thread canvas 20 x 20in (50 x 50cm)
• Size 18 tapestry needle
• ½yd (50cm) of fabric for backing and matching sewing thread
• 12in (30cm) zipper
• 1¾yd (1.6m) of multicolored ready-made cord for edging
• Four 3in (7.5cm) gold tassels for corners
• Pillow form slightly larger than finished needlepoint design
Design size: 14 x 14in (35.5 x 35.5cm)

WORKING THE DESIGN
The chart is 140 stitches wide and 140 stitches high. Using a single strand of tapestry yarn, work the design in tent stitch. The color key gives the main uses of each color. See page 114 for tent-stitch techniques, blocking and finishing instructions, and technical tips.

COLOR KEY
This design was made in Appleton (Ap) tapestry yarn. Alternative yarns listed on page 124 will give a slightly different effect.

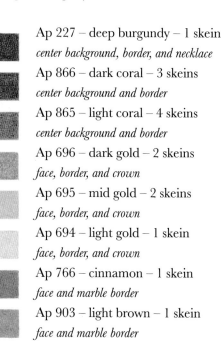

Ap 227 – deep burgundy – 1 skein
center background, border, and necklace

Ap 866 – dark coral – 3 skeins
center background and border

Ap 865 – light coral – 4 skeins
center background and border

Ap 696 – dark gold – 2 skeins
face, border, and crown

Ap 695 – mid gold – 2 skeins
face, border, and crown

Ap 694 – light gold – 1 skein
face, border, and crown

Ap 766 – cinnamon – 1 skein
face and marble border

Ap 903 – light brown – 1 skein
face and marble border

Ap 244 – dark olive green – 2 skeins
key pattern and marble borders

Ap 333 – light olive green – 1 skein
key pattern and marble borders

Ap 832 – dark jade green – 2 skeins
border

Ap 831 – light jade green – 3 skeins
necklace and border

Ap 935 – deep grape – 2 skeins
hair, eyes, and border

Ap 588 – deep brown – 2 skeins
hair, eyes, border, eyebrows, and mouth

Ap 976 – dark taupe – 1 skein
face and marble border

Ap 973 – light taupe – 1 skein
face and marble border

Ap 691 – light beige – 2 skeins
eyes, earring, and border patterns

COPTIC GOD AND GODDESS

I love textile fragments. Scraps like these seem to carry a greater significance than a whole piece, and make me feel fortunate that I am being allowed a glimpse into antiquity.

This Coptic woven tapestry was the inspiration for my God and Goddess cushion. It is not truly pagan, for the Copts were the first to adopt Christianity in Egypt, in the 1st century AD, but it celebrates both Pan, the half-animal pagan god of flocks and herds, who amused himself by "panicking" men and women who found themselves in lonely spots, and Dionysus, the god of wine, fertility, and pleasures of the flesh.

I have altered the original design source a little, to depict a haloed god and goddess, he still half-animal, half-human, she dressed in a leopard skin. She is touching her consort's shoulder, suggesting both mutual companionship and inter-dependence. Together they are full of earthy vitality and joy. Floating on the wine-dark of the background are ancient symbols pertaining to the male and female.

The triangle is one of the earliest symbols of all. It represents the regenerative womb of the great earth goddess and her triple aspect as maiden, mother, crone. The snake is associated with immortality: every year it sloughs off its old skin, emerging anew, just as a woman sheds the lining of her womb. Shown winding vertically upward, the snake represents the life force.

Crescere is the Latin for "to grow," and the crescent (or waxing) moon suggests growth, productivity, creation. Wavy lines represent water, the source of all life: the element in which the unborn baby lies in the womb.

In addition to these, I show a circle, conveying the concentrated energy of the center; two dots, representing the strength of two; three columns, denoting the totality of the trinity; and the horns of a ram to symbolize masculinity.

Finally, the border of my Coptic cushion has rows of petals that meet in the center, opening buds that represent the unfolding mysteries of life and love.

The Coptic God and Goddess (right), and a late 3rd-century Egyptian textile fragment of Dionysus and Pan (above)

*A*nd they were both naked, the man and his wife, and were not ashamed.

THE BIBLE, GENESIS, 2.25

*W*hen Ridjalu l'Ghabib wanted to shape the woman's body, he took the roundness of the moon, the pliancy of the snake, the twining embrace of the lianas, the trembling of the grass, the quivering of the cane, the perfume of the flowers, the lightness and agility of the leaves, the glance of the doe, the gaiety and charm of the sunlight, the swiftness of the wind, the tears of the clouds, the delicacy of the feather, the shyness of the small bird, the sweetness of honey, the vanity of the peacock, the slimness of the swallow, the beauty of the the diamond, and the cooing of the turtle dove.

THE CREATION OF WOMAN, A MALAY MYTH

MAKING THE CUSHION

MATERIALS

- Appleton tapestry yarn in 9 colors
- 10-mesh ecru double-thread canvas 18 x 18in (45 x 45cm)
- Size 18 tapestry needle
- ½yd (50cm) of fabric for backing and matching sewing thread
- 10in (25cm) zipper
- 2¼yd (2m) of ready-made cord (enough for twists at corners)
- Four large toggles for corners
- Pillow form slightly larger than finished needlepoint design

Design size: 12 x 12in (30.5 x 30.5cm)

WORKING THE DESIGN

The chart is 120 stitches wide and 120 stitches high. Using a single strand of tapestry yarn, work the design in tent stitch. The color key gives the main uses of each color. See page 114 for tent-stitch techniques, blocking and finishing instructions, and technical tips.

COLOR KEY

This design was made in Appleton (Ap) tapestry yarn. Alternative yarns listed on page 124 will give a slightly different effect.

Ap 694 – golden yellow – 3 skeins
hearts, god, goddess, etc.

Ap 294 – dark green – 2 skeins
hearts, god's legs, outer border stripe, etc.

Ap 355 – grass green – 1 skein
god and goddess

Ap 354 – light green – 1 skein
goddess, snake, etc.

Ap 155 – blue – 2 skeins
water symbol, hearts, etc.

Ap 934 – deep grape – 5 skeins
background only

Ap 767 – dark cinnamon – 1 skein
hearts, god and goddess outlines, and hair

Ap 765 – mid cinnamon – 3 skeins
hearts, god, goddess, etc.

Ap 764 – light cinnamon – 3 skeins
hearts, god, goddess, etc.

Detail of an angel from a 4th-century Coptic textile (above)

COURTLY LOVE

*T*he love celebrated by the trouba-
dours of southern France in the
twelfth century was passionate, ennobling,
chivalrous, religious in its intensity—and
ever unfulfilled. No valiant knight would
be without his fair lady, waiting devotedly
in fortified fairytale splendor for his
return from the noble deeds that were
to transform him into a fearless warrior
and to prove him worthy
of her love.

*The Renaissance Heart (left), an ornate love
token, inspired by this 16th-century fabric,
enriched with flowers, beads, and gold threads*

Come, O come, my life's delight,
Let me not in languor pine:
Love loves no delay; thy sight,
The more enjoyed, the more divine:
O come, and take from me
The pain of being deprived of thee.

A LITTLE WORLD,
THOMAS CAMPION (1567–1620)

SIGNOR MARSILIO AND HIS
WIFE *(below), by Lorenzo Lotto*
(1480–1556)

Courtly love demanded sacrifice, courage, adventure, romance, and poetry. The passionate story of Tristan and Isolde was echoed in other medieval tales where love was ele-vated to a supreme and sacred level. Courtship became an ideal, a poetic attitude, a private sport of the aristocracy, an end in itself. Accomplishments were required: skill at riding, fencing, archery, hunting, tournaments, singing, and versifying. Battles were fought gallantly, for love; dragons were slain; turreted castles were taken; and knights set out on the quest of the Holy Grail.

By the time of the Renaissance, love and marriage ceased to be seen as mutually exclusive. Romantic impulse was tempered by the demands of power and property, leading to all the pomp and circumstance of dynastic marriages. Women were no longer symbols of man's imagining, but were appreciated for their cultivated intellect and their abilities, as well as for their moral virtue and sexual attraction. The explosion of intellectual, artistic, and scientific activity throughout Europe at this time affected everyone. Women were admired for their beauty, and although their symbolic associations with goddesses continued, they were loved also for their womanhood, as able partners. This was love on a human plane. "Love," wrote Shakespeare, "comforteth like sunshine after rain."

My love in her attire doth show her wit,
it doth so well become her
For every season she hath dressings fit,
For Winter, Spring and Summer.
No beauty she doth miss
When all her robes are on:
But beauty's self she is
When all her robes are gone.

ANON. (1602)

A true love longs for
the embraces
of the loved one only.
*A lover pales at the sight
of his beloved.
Love can deny love
nothing.*

TWELFTH-CENTURY
CODES OF LOVE,
ANON.

LUCREZIA BORGIA *(left), the
celebrated beauty of Renaissance
Italy, by Bartolomeo da Venezia
(1502–1546)*

FLORENTINE ANGEL

My musical Angel evokes the Renaissance, the religious inspiration that lay behind the creativity in art, music, and architecture, and its chalky colors are Florentine—soft rose, burnt sienna, ocher, vermillion, and raw umber. The wings of medieval angels are as varied and fabulous as birds' wings, and each is embellished with gold. I have placed the word *Amor* on my swirling scrolls, animating the blue-green space around the angel, the symbol of God's love.

Love is my life, life is my love,
Love is my whole felicity,
Love is my sweet, sweet is my love,
I am in love, and love is in me.

THE SHEPHERD'S GARLAND,
MICHAEL DRAYTON (1563–1631)

Detail from a door panel (below), by Francesco Botticini (c. 1446–1497), and the Florentine Angel (right)

My inspiration was a decorated door panel by Botticini, on which a row of angels, feet delicately placed on a celestial heaven, play medieval instruments—viols, horns, mandolins, triangles, and trumpets. I chose one angel, playing a tambourine. Could this angel be waiting on St Cecilia, the patron saint of music?

Unfortunately, it is impossible to translate the delicate features of these heavenly beings on such a small scale into needlepoint, but at least I was able to choose wool threads that captured the milky and soft tones of this delicate sacred decoration.

The rich border is from another painting on wood that awakens for me the glories of the age. I felt it made an appropriate surrounding for the heavenly vision within.

Angels today have become symbolic of all kinds of love, and of course they combine elements of the ancient winged mythological god, Eros, and the cupids of the Roman times. As messengers they intercede between divine powers and the mortals below. Secular society has embraced angels as symbols of love and purity, while the Christian religion will always perceive them as the appointed bringers of "comfort and joy."

I painted one of my favorite quotations from Shakespeare's *Hamlet* onto the steps in my cottage for my son to see at night before he goes to bed: "Goodnight Sweet Prince, and flights of Angels sing thee to thy Rest."

MAKING THE CUSHION

*A*nd what is better
than wisedoom?
*Womman. And what is
better than a good
womman? Nothyng.*

THE TALE OF MELIBEE,
GEOFFREY CHAUCER
(1345–1400)

or two strands of gold metallic thread, work
the design in tent stitch. The color key gives
the main uses of each color. See page 114 for
tent-stitch techniques and technical tips.

COLOR KEY

This design was made in Appleton (Ap) tapestry yarn. Alternative yarns listed on page 124
will give a slightly different effect.

Ap 208 – deep brick red – 1 skein
wings, hair band, and tambourine

Ap 726 – dark coral – 6 skeins
border and gown shading

Ap 865 – mid coral – 4 skeins
border and gown

Ap 721 – light terracotta – 1 skein
wings, mouth, and cheeks

Ap 696 – dark mustard – 6 skeins
border and hair

Ap 695 – mid mustard – 4 skeins
border, hair, and tambourine

Ap 314 – olive green – 2 skeins
border outline and wings

Ap 342 – light green – 3 skeins
background crosses only

Ap 822 – royal blue – 1 skein
sleeves, wings, and eyes

Ap 154 – light blue – 7 skeins
center background only

Ap 974 – taupe – 2 skeins
face and scrolls

Ap 761 – beige – 3 skeins
face, hands, scrolls, and background dots

gold metallic thread – 1 ball
wings, tambourine, and gown patterns

MATERIALS
• Appleton tapestry yarn in 12 colors and
Twilley's *Goldfingering* (metallic thread) in gold
• 10-mesh ecru double-thread canvas 20 x
20in (49 x 49cm)
• Size 18 tapestry needle
• ½yd (50cm) of fabric for backing and
matching sewing thread
• 11in (28cm) zipper
• 1¾yd (1.6m) of ready-made cord
• Four 3in (7.5cm) gold tassels
• Pillow form slightly larger than design
Design size: 13½ x 13½ in (34 x 34cm)

WORKING THE DESIGN
The chart is 135 stitches wide and 135 stitches high. Using a single strand of tapestry yarn,

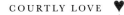

VENUS'S ROBE

Botticelli's *Birth of Venus* is a picture alive with allegory, a powerful and mystical celebration of love and beauty coming to humanity. Venus signifies the sexual and spiritual powers of love and is welcomed to the shore by one of the three Horae. The four elements of life are said to be reflected in the painting—water, air (she is blown to shore by the winds), earth, and fire (symbolized by the flame-like locks of golden hair).

The three interlocking corn-flowers on the dress of one of Venus's Horae were the inspiration for this design, and the pattern of daisies against the shell pink background, as well as the inner border, come from the beautiful mantle she is holding for the goddess of love as she emerges naked from the foam. Such delicate flowers suggest a freshness and inno-cence, while Venus herself radiates the glory and mystery of love as she lands in a scallop shell on the shore. This shell, with its two tightly hinged parts, was a common symbol of passionate sexual love.

There are many interpreta-tions of the allegory within this picture, with some defining Venus as spiritual and others as sexual love. For me, Botticelli's radiant Venus was the embodiment of humanity, born to civ-ilization, and she signifies the beauty of love. She is welcomed on the shore by Nature, who clothes and provides for her.

*B**eauty, like truth, shines most in nakedness.*

ANON. (1727)

Venus's Robe cushion (left), inspired by a flower detail from THE BIRTH OF VENUS *(above), by Sandro Botticelli (c. 1445–1510)*

MAKING THE CUSHION

MATERIALS

- Appleton tapestry yarn in 8 colors and Twilley's *Goldfingering* (metallic thread) in gold
- 10-mesh ecru double-thread canvas 19 x 19in (48 x 48cm)
- Size 18 tapestry needle
- ½yd (50cm) of fabric for backing and matching sewing thread
- 11in (28cm) zipper
- 1¾yd (1.6m) of ready-made gold cord
- Four 7.5cm (3in) gold tassels
- Pillow form slightly larger than finished needlepoint design

Design size: 13 x 13in (33 x 33cm)

WORKING THE DESIGN

The chart is 130 stitches wide and 130 stitches high. Using a single strand of tapestry yarn, or two strands of gold metallic thread, work the design in tent stitch. The color key gives the main uses of each color. See page 114 for tent-stitch techniques, blocking and finishing instructions, and technical tips.

COLOR KEY

This design was made in Appleton (Ap) tapestry yarn. Alternative yarns listed on page 124 will give a slightly different effect.

Ap 205 – dark rose pink – 6 skeins
border background

Ap 222 – light rose pink – 7 skeins
border background

Ap 472 – yellow – 1 skein
centers of daisies only

Ap 851 – cream – 2 skeins
inner border

Ap 358 – dark green – 4 skeins
leaves and stems

Ap 314 – olive green – 2 skeins
leaves and stems

Ap 745 – blue – 1 skein
cornflowers

Ap 991 – white – 5 skeins
center background and daisies

gold metallic thread – 1 ball
inner border

Detail from map of Italy (below), by Danti Ignazio (1536–1586)

MEDIEVAL CORNFLOWER

The Medieval Cornflower (right), and its source (below), a detail from a medieval illuminated manuscript from CARDINAL WOLSEY'S EPISTLE BOOK, *c. 1500*

In the medieval flower garden, every plant was charged with hidden significance. There is an appealing myth associated with the cornflower: a sad youth, Cyanus (which is the botanical name for the cornflower to this day) so loved flowers that he made wreaths of them all day long. His favorite was the cornflower, and he longed to be clothed in garments of the same astonishing blue. One day he was found dead among his adored flowers, and the goddess Flora, out of respect for his devotion to her, changed him into his favorite flower.

Yet flowers were imbued with more than just mythical significance. Within the quiet walls of the various religious orders, the botanical study of plants flourished, and medicinal and practical qualities of stems, roots, and seeds were soon well documented. The monks who carefully tended their herbariums grew species that would cure diseases, relieve dizziness, prevent colds, and soothe their toothache.

Wild and garden flowers were skillfully recorded on the pages of their illuminated manuscripts, and

Foure things cannot be kept close, Love, the cough, fyre and sorrowe.

THE GARDEN OF PLEASURE, J. SANFORDE (1573)

O Western wind, when wilt thou blow, That the small rain down can rain? Christ, that my love were in my arms And I in my bed again!

THE LOVER IN WINTER PLAINETH FOR THE SPRING, ANON. (C. 1530)

this cornflower painting, with its lapis lazuli petals and slender leaves placed on a complementary golden-yellow background, is one such decoration. Its strength of color and simplicity made it an ideal subject.

I carried the intense blue to the border, decorated it with strawberries, and sprinkled it with dots of gold. Strawberries were used for whitening the teeth in medieval times, but they also had erotic connotations with their rich colors and multitude of seeds. They were also considered "food for the blessed"; decorative and symbolic, they appeared often in medieval tapestries.

The medieval Dutch painter, Hieronymus Bosch, uses the strawberry repeatedly in his imaginative *Garden of Earthly Delights*. This surreal and futuristic work (see page 45) forms a triptych representing Heaven, Earth, and Hell. The panel for Hell depicts men and women devouring or expelling huge strawberries. To this deeply religious painter, the strawberry symbolized the sexual act, with its luscious red form, and its promise of fleeting sensory pleasure. Yet, the meticulous detailing of his imaginings suggests an obsessive preoccupation with dark and erotic delights.

*A*nd I will make thee
beds of roses
And a thousand
fragrant posies
A cap of flowers,
and a kirtle
Embroidered all with
leaves of myrtle.

CHRISTOPHER MARLOWE
(1564–1593)

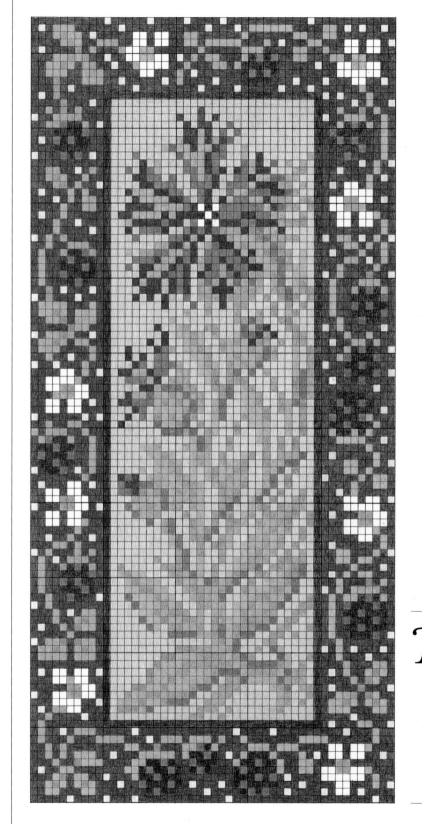

*T*hus all, sweet Fair,
in time must have
an end,
Except thy beauty,
virtues, and thy friend.

GILES FLETCHER
(1588–1623)

MAKING THE PURSE OR PICTURE

MATERIALS

• Appleton tapestry yarn in 10 colors and
Twilley's *Goldfingering* (metallic thread) in gold
• 10-mesh ecru double-thread canvas 11 x
16in (28 x 41cm)
• Size 18 tapestry needle
• Small piece of fabric for back of purse and
for lining, and matching sewing thread
• 2½yd (2.3m) of ready-made cord
• Two 3¾in (9.5cm) burgundy tassels
Design size: 5 x 10½ in (13 x 26.5cm)

WORKING THE DESIGN

The chart is 50 stitches wide and 105 stitches high. Using a single strand of tapestry yarn,
or two strands of gold metallic thread, work
the design in tent stitch. The color key gives
the main uses of each color. Note also that the
shading on the center background is worked
in 696 and 695. The centers of the large
flowers are worked in 948. See page 121 or
122 for finishing instructions.

COLOR KEY

This design was made in Appleton (Ap) tapestry yarn. Alternative yarns listed on page 124
will give a slightly different effect.

 Ap 948 – strawberry – 1 skein
strawberries and inner border

Ap 696 – dark gold – 1 skein
strawberry seeds

Ap 695 – mid gold – 1 skein
daisy centers

Ap 694 – light gold – 2 skeins
center background

Ap 355 – olive green – 1 skein
leaves and stems

Ap 831 – jade green – 2 skeins
leaves and stems

Ap 823 – dark blue – 2 skeins
border background and center flowers

Ap 464 – mid blue – 1 skein
center flowers

Ap 463 – light blue – 1 skein
center flowers

Ap 871 – cream – 1 skein
border flowers

gold metallic thread – 1 ball
border dots only

Detail from GARDEN OF
EARTHLY DELIGHTS
*(above), by Hieronymous Bosch
(1450–1516)*

RENAISSANCE HEART

The Renaissance Heart, an ornate love token encrusted with red and green beads (right), and a detail from THE TENDER TOUCH *(below), by Eleanor Fortescue Brickdale (1871–1945)*

*All soft and sweet the maid appears,
With looks that know no art,
And though she yields with
trembling fears,
She yields with all her heart.*

THE EMPEROR OF THE MOON,
APHRA BENN (1640–1689)

This is my favorite design. I love it because it oozes deep passion. My inspiration came (once again) from the Victoria & Albert Museum, which always stimulates me. I stand there among the wealth of treasures in awe, and always come away with the desire to create wonderful things.

This time, it was a deep maroon embroidered satin of 1575 that inspired me. Stylized flowers and leaves were worked in metal threads and faded colored silks, and heart shapes were fitted one into the other over the fabric. I decided to take just one heart and fill it with the most loved flowers of the Renaissance period.

The bluebell (which is found on the body of the unicorn in the famous "Lady and the Unicorn" tapestry) implies fertility, and it was a popular belief that "bluebells suspended whole above the threshold, all evil things would flee therefrom." A carpet of bluebells in spring woodland is still one of the most heavenly and breathtaking sights. The tiny modest violet, with its heart-shaped leaves, is found in most of the *millefleur* tapestries and supposedly covered the ground in the Garden of Eden. Though humble, its purple color is the color of royalty, and its sweet odor is said to refresh the spirit.

In the center is the Tudor rose, best loved of all medieval flowers. Roses were believed to have grown thorns only after the Fall, and the rose with its thorns also represented Christ's wounds, and became a symbol of martyrdom. Roses were also associated with the cult of flowers dedicated to the Virgin Mary. Popularly, they have always represented the beloved and stood for sensual pleasure.

For your youth excuses you from being very wise, and will still excuse you in everything that you do with good intent to please me. And know that it doth not displease, but rather pleases me that you should have roses to grow and violets to care for and that you should make chaplets and dance and sing…

MEDIEVAL PEOPLE,
LE MENAGERIER DE PARIS

Shakespeare also mentioned his favorite bloom, the rose, more times than any other flower in his plays. In *The Taming of the Shrew* Petruchio declares his plan to woo the shrewish Kate: "I'll say she looks as clear as morning roses newly washed with dew."

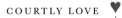

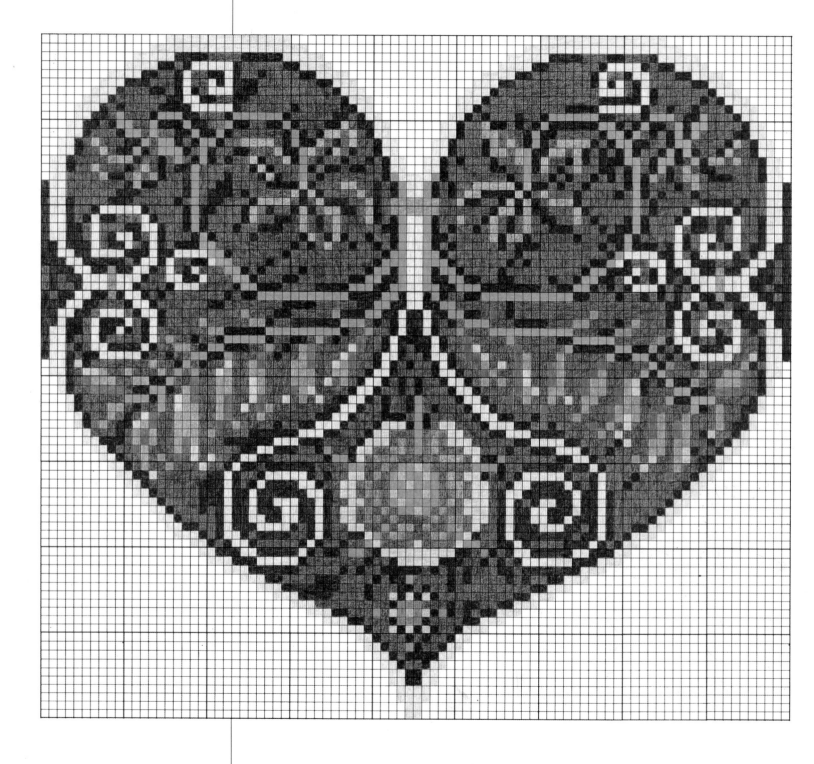

MAKING THE PINCUSHION

MATERIALS

- Anchor Marlitt *Viscose Rayon* (or cotton embroidery thread) in 13 colors and *Madeira Metallic Effect* Yarn in 3 shades
- 10-mesh ecru double-thread canvas 15 x 14in (38 x 35cm)
- Size 18 tapestry needle
- Small piece of fabric for backing and matching sewing thread
- 1yd (1m) of ⅝in (1.5cm) wide burgundy braid (or ribbon) for edging
- One 3¼in (8cm) gold tassel
- 14 burgundy bobbles for trimming the braid and 70 small glass beads in a mixture of green and rose pink
- One 3¼in (8cm) gold tassel
- Two pieces of thick cardboard same size as finished needlepoint design
- Padding

Design size: 9 x 8in (23 x 20cm)

WORKING THE DESIGN

The chart is 90 stitches wide and 80 stitches high. Mount the canvas on an embroidery frame to ensure that it will retain its shape. Using two strands of rayon, or three strands of fine metallic thread (one strand of each shade), work the design in tent stitch. The color key gives the main uses of each color. See page 121 for pincushion finishing instructions. To make your own tassel, follow the steps on page 120.

As true a lover, as ever sigh'd upon a midnight pillow.

AS YOU LIKE IT,
WILLIAM SHAKESPEARE
(1564–1616)

COLOR KEY

This design was made in Marlitt (Mt) rayon and Madeira (Ma) metallic thread. Cotton embroidery thread can be used instead of the rayon, and the suggested color equivalents are given on page 124.

Mt 1211 – deep burgundy – 3 skeins
background shading

Mt 1209 – dusky rose – 5 skeins
background

Mt 881 – mid rose pink – 1 skein
tudor rose

Mt 830 – light rose pink – 1 skein
tudor rose

Mt 1019 – pastel rose pink – 1 skein
tudor rose outline

Mt 1079 – golden yellow – 1 skein
flower centers

Mt 1146 – green – 1 skein
stems, leaves, and rose center

Mt 836 – dark blue – 1 skein
bluebells

Mt 835 – mid blue – 1 skein
bluebells

Mt 1009 – light blue – 1 skein
bluebells

Mt 859 – dark violet – 1 skein
violets

Mt 858 – mid violet – 1 skein
violets

Mt 857 – light violet – 1 skein
violets

Ma 5014, 5011, and 5017 – 1 each
decorative swirls and border

The ornately embroidered 16th-century fabric from the Victoria & Albert Museum (below), the inspiration for the Renaissance Heart pincushion

REGENCY ROMPS

*I*n a period famous for its sparkling
wit and polished surface, love was
an elaborate game; a diversion, a sport.
The vulgarity, promiscuity, and excesses
of the Georgian underbelly were tightly
corseted by social ritual. Obsessed with
the pursuit of pleasure and amusement,
Georgians enjoyed the intrigue, the
scandal and the minutiae of amorous
anticipation, persuasion,
and conquest.

The Forget-me-not Teapot cushion (left), sur-
rounded by summer flowers, and a detail (above)
from the Minton book of teawares, c. 1799

*A*myntas led me to a grove
Where all the trees
did shade us:
The sun itself, though it had strove,
Yet could not have betrayed us.
The place, secure from human eyes,
No other fear allows,
But when the winds that gently rise
Do kiss the yielding boughs.

APHRA BEHN (1640–1689)

THE SWING *(right) and* THE
STOLEN KISS *(below), both
by Jean Honoré Fragonard
(1732–1806)*

Behind the gracefully regimented and classically proportioned façades of Georgian terraces and crescents, drawing rooms were tastefully elegant and sparsely furnished. Chippendale tables were adorned with snuff boxes and decorative porcelain; minuets were played on harpsichords and flutes; and ladies gossiped together as they sat at their sewing. Social life was punctuated with elaborate, highly artificial masquerades, with taking tea, and with much fluttering of hearts and fans.

Georgian England was reacting to the less sophisticated attitudes, religious fervor, and political turmoil of the preceding centuries. In the Age of Reason and Enlightenment life was ordered, rational, and based on scientific principles. Love was a far cry from the mystical, courtly, idealized love practiced in the Middle Ages.

Deep feelings were sacrificed to a code of manners in which expressions of love were literary toys, full of polite trifles, polished conceits, and affected gallantries. There was much self-conscious wooing and practiced sighing by the perfectly composed and delicately mannered ladies. Love was essentially frivolous. A pastime. A human folly. The aim was to entertain, to fascinate, and to win.

Horace Walpole's cynical wit seems to me to sum up the Georgian period: "The world is Comedy to those who think, a Tragedy to those who feel."

*B*e not ever then repining,
Sighing, dying,
canting, whining,
Spend not time in vain pursuing;
If she does not love, make her;
When she loves you, then – forsake her;
'Tis the modish way of wooing.

POEMS ON SEVERAL OCCASIONS,
HENRY CAREY (1693–1743)

GEORGIAN VEST

Like the illuminated borders of medieval manuscripts, the Georgian vest delights in the enchanted world of Nature. All manner of flowers and insects are captured on the cloth, with the charm and delicacy of a spring garden.

Wandering through museums of costume, I am inevitably attracted to the embroidered details on stockings, night caps, gloves, shoes, and purses. The vest of the Regency beau is always the most sumptuously embroidered of all, with its fabric—in the pastel colors of sugared almonds—flowered with blossoms and sprigs of greenery.

In a book of French vest details that my assistant gave me, I was delighted to find a *trompe l'œil* lapel with a small bunch of flowers through the buttonhole. This transformed my ideas for my vest. Instead of a formal, traditional design, I quickly decided on a more quirky creation. I chose a soft custard yellow for the background, a warm terracotta for the pockets and lapels, and just let myself go in arranging all my favorite flowers. I added two further motifs to the *trompe l'œil* pockets, the dragonfly and the Greek urn—details that delight the eye rather than deceive it. To complete the romantic effect, I scattered flowers and positioned trailing swirls, snails, moths, and butterflies down the edges and over the warm yellow background.

> *I*'ll make a strawy garland,
> *I'll make it wondrous fine,*
> *With roses, lilies, daisies,*
> *I'll mix the eglantine;*
> *And I'll present it to my love*
> *when he returns from sea*
> *For I love my love, because*
> *I know my love loves me.*
>
> 18TH CENTURY BALLAD, ANON.

The Georgian vest being stitched (right), and a detail (above) of a late 18th-century French watercolor of the original vest that inspired this needlepoint design

*F*aces painted pink
and brown;
*Waistcoats strip'd
and gaudy.*

MODERN MALE FASHIONS,
MARY ROBINSON (1800)

The Georgian vest, photographed in the Royal Pavilion, Brighton, England (left)

MAKING THE VEST

MATERIALS
- Appleton tapestry yarn in 15 colors
- 12-mesh cream or white interlock canvas 32 x 28in (81 x 71cm)
- Size 18 tapestry needle
- 1yd (90cm) of 36in (91cm) wide fabric for back and matching sewing thread
- 2yd (1.8m) of 36in (91cm) wide fabric for lining and matching sewing thread
- 2¼yd (2m) of narrow cord for edging
- Buckle for back belt and 3 globe buttons

Design size: approximately 39in (98cm) around bust/chest at underarm and 22¼in (56cm) from shoulder to pointed lower edge

COLOR KEY

This design was made in Appleton (Ap) tapestry yarn. See Color Key on next page for yarn amounts and color uses.

Ap 947
strawberry

Ap 945
pink

Ap 721
terracotta

Ap 623
orange

Ap 473
gold

Ap 471
custard yellow

Ap 543
green

Ap 541
light gray-green

Ap 525
turquoise

Ap 822
dark blue

Ap 463
light blue

Ap 893
lilac

Ap 454
violet

Ap 967
charcoal

Ap 992
white

WORKING THE DESIGN

Each chart is 120 stitches across the widest point and 268 stitches across the longest point. Mount the canvas on an embroidery frame to ensure that it will retain its shape. Turn the chart so that it is the right way up, and using a single strand of tapestry yarn, work the design in tent stitch. The color key on pages 58 and 59 gives the main uses of each color. Note that shade 967 (charcoal) is also used for the strawberry seeds, the snail, the insects, and on some flowers. See page 116 for the various tent-stitch techniques and page 122 for vest finishing instructions.

COLOR KEY

This design was made in Appleton (Ap) tapestry yarn. Alternative yarns listed on page 124 will give a slightly different effect than the one shown in the picture on page 55.

 Ap 947 – strawberry – 1 skein
strawberries and some flowers

Ap 945 – pink – 2 skeins
pocket outline, strawberries, and flowers

Ap 721 – terracotta – 6 skeins
lapels, pockets flaps, and some flowers

Ap 623 – orange – 1 skein
snails and some flowers

Ap 473 – gold – 1 skein
some flowers centers, urn, and insects

 Ap 471 – custard yellow – 27 skeins
background, urn, and dragonfly's head

Ap 543 – green – 3 skeins
stems, leaves, and moth

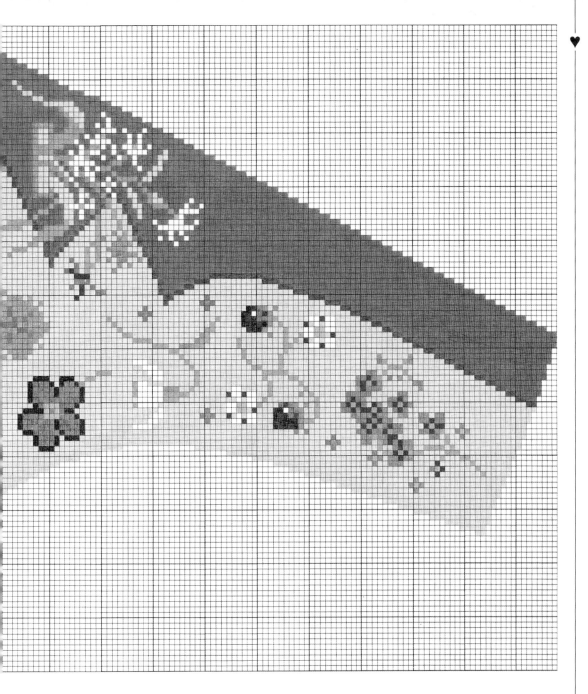

A delicate textile design with trailing sprigs of summer flowers (above), by William Kilburn (1745–1818)

Ap 541 – light gray-green – 1 skein
some flowers, leaves, etc.

Ap 525 – turquoise – 2 skeins
curlicues, leaves, stems, and flowers

Ap 822 – dark blue – 2 skeins
blue flowers and urn

Ap 463 – light blue – 2 skeins
blue flowers, urn, and insects

Ap 893 – lilac – 3 skeins
snails, urn, some flowers, and buttonhole

Ap 454 – violet – 1 skein
bars on curlicues and some flowers

Ap 967 – charcoal – 2 skeins
lapel and pocket flap outlines

Ap 992 – white – 2 skeins
some flowers and insects

TOILE DE JOUY CUPIDS

"Oh, that wanton boy with darts of Love, and fluttering wings!" Since ancient times, Cupid has hovered over courting couples, complete with phallic arrows and a swarm of bees to symbolize the sweetness and sting of love. The youngest of the gods, Cupid caused suffering to men and gods by his malicious pranks. Today, he is little more than a chubby, mischievous archer, but the prick of his darts still arouse passion in all who feel them.

It was nevertheless Eros (the Greek name for Cupid) who, when ordered by the jealous Aphrodite, goddess of love, to punish the mortal Psyche for her beauty and deliver her up to a monster, taught Psyche the joys of tenderness and love. Visiting her only during the hours of darkness (his bow and arrows laid neatly at the foot of the bed), he made her swear never to attempt to see his face. But curiosity got the better of her, and Psyche held a lamp to his face. Drops of hot oil falling on his shoulders awoke Eros, who, reproaching Psyche for her lack of trust, vanished. Psyche suffered terrible trials, but Eros continued to cherish and protect her, and eventually persuaded Zeus to allow her to rejoin him. The wedding of the two lovers was celebrated on Olympus with feasting and rejoicing.

The charming 18th-century designs of Toile de Jouy fabric are mostly based on finely engraved scenes from provincial life, with young girls on swings, pieces of architecture,

The gray Toile de Jouy Cupid cushion (right), and the original engraving which was my starting point (above)

trees, monkeys, parrots, and dogs. And, of course, little flying Cupids! Colors are monochrome on a white background. Pink was the favorite, from madder "fixed" with cow dung, but blue from the indigo plant, sepia, black, and violet were all used.

The Indian technique of printing onto cotton cloth was adapted by the Toile de Jouy factory at Jouy-en-Josas near Versailles toward the end of the 18th century, and their fabrics quickly became the height of Regency fashion.

---

*T*he wingèd boy draws near,
  And thus the swain reproves,
While beauty revell'd here,
My game lay in the groves;
  At Court I never fail
To scatter round my arrows,
Men fall as thick as hail;
And maidens love like sparrows.

DAMON AND CUPID, JOHN GAY (1685–1782)

The source for my own Toile design was just a small engraving of a cupid from a decoupage book. The lines were simple and strong—thus perfect for adapting to needlepoint. I also liked the fact that he is carrying his bow and arrow, and the swirling ribbons suggest he is in flight.

Using 12-mesh canvas to capture the fine lines, I first worked the design in cream and gray, then decided to experiment with the other colorways. All four cushions go well together, or you could make two in the same colorway to adorn your Georgian *chaise longue*.

MAKING THE CUSHION

MATERIALS

- Appleton tapestry yarn in 3 colors
- 12-mesh ecru double-thread canvas 15 x 18in (38 x 44cm) for each cushion
- Size 18 tapestry needle
- Small piece of fabric for backing and matching sewing thread
- 8in (21cm) zipper
- 1¼yd (1.2m) of ready-made cord for each of the cushions
- Four 2¾in (7cm) tassels for each cushion
- Pillow form slightly larger than design

Design size: 9 x 11½ in (23 x 29cm)

WORKING THE DESIGN

The chart is 108 stitches wide and 138 stitches high. Using a single strand of tapestry yarn, work the design in tent stitch. The color keys give the main uses of each color. Note that the inner background color is also used for the swirls and dots in the outer background. See page 114 for technical tips.

The blue colorway for the Toile de Jouy Cupid cushion (right), and alternative colorways (pages 64 and 65)

COLOR KEYS

These designs were made in Appleton (Ap) tapestry yarn. Alternative yarns listed on page 124 will give a slightly different effect than the one shown in the picture on pages 64 and 65.

Blue colorway

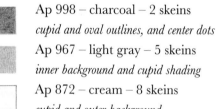

Ap 568 – dark blue – 2 skeins
cupid and oval outlines, and center dots

Ap 464 – sky blue – 5 skeins
inner background and cupid shading

Ap 872 – cream – 8 skeins
cupid and outer background

Gray colorway

Ap 998 – charcoal – 2 skeins
cupid and oval outlines, and center dots

Ap 967 – light gray – 5 skeins
inner background and cupid shading

Ap 872 – cream – 8 skeins
cupid and outer background

Green colorway

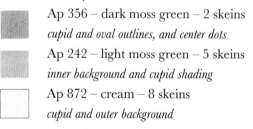

Ap 356 – dark moss green – 2 skeins
cupid and oval outlines, and center dots

Ap 242 – light moss green – 5 skeins
inner background and cupid shading

Ap 872 – cream – 8 skeins
cupid and outer background

Red colorway

Ap 149 – dark raspberry – 2 skeins
cupid and oval outlines, and center dots

Ap 226 – light raspberry – 5 skeins
inner background and cupid shading

Ap 872 – cream – 8 skeins
cupid and outer background

AUBUSSON ROSES

*Come, let us now resolve at last
To live and love in quiet;
We'll tie the knot so very fast
That Time shall ne'er untie it.*

THE RECONCILEMENT, JOHN SHEFFIELD,
DUKE OF BUCKINGHAM (1648–1721)

The Aubusson Roses chair seat (right), and a detail from THE EMBROIDERY LESSON *(below), by Madeleine Lemaire (1845–1928)*

Walking along the streets of New York City, I once saw in a window a sophisticated cushion made from a fragment of woven tapestry. As a weaver myself, and understanding the com-

plexities, I am always stunned by the the sheer mastery of the craft of tapestry. That cushion was evocative of an early chintz textile design, and had for me the beauty of a full-blown summer's day.

I used this tapestry fragment for the starting point for the Aubusson Roses chair seat but changed the background from white to a delicate yellow, to give it a more Georgian mood, and tied some small sprays of flowers with a ribbon, to add interest in the corners.

It was the lushness and the open bloom of the peonies, phlox, and roses that I was most intent on capturing in my design. The rose is the emblem of Venus, goddess of love, and has long featured in the language of love. The goddess's flower is exulted in Dodeon's *History of Plants* (1578): "Ye shall also find this written of roses, that at the first they were all white, and that they became red afterward with the blood of the Goddess Venus…"

With its beauty, its intoxicating scent and sharp thorns (to protect virginity), the rose has since earliest times represented the wonder and pangs of new love.

The silky blue ribbon was added to make a graceful border but it is also a *trompe l'œil* device that fools the eye into thinking there is a real ribbon there.

Blue ribbons have always been linked with the goddess Hera, protector of marriage and fidelity. Blue is traditionally the color associated with the Virgin Mary. It has been a time-honored custom for lovers to wear a blue token to symbolize love that transcends sexual attraction, while a tied ribbon signifies the marriage of body and soul.

*Fairest of the stitching train,
Ease my passion by your art;
And, in pity to my pain,
Mend the hole that's in my heart.*

TO A SEMPSTRESS, ANON. (1727)

MAKING THE CHAIR SEAT

Detail from the painting
PORTRAIT OF QUEEN
MARIE-ANTOINETTE
(above), by Louise Elisabeth
Vigée-Lebrun (1755–1842)

MATERIALS
• Appleton tapestry yarn in the 19 colors listed below in the color key
• 10-mesh white double-thread canvas at least 24in (61cm) square or 3in (7.5cm) bigger all around than desired finished size of the chair-seat cover
• Size 18 tapestry needle
• Template for chair seat
• Ready-made cord for edging
Design size without extra background added outside ribbon: 17¼ x 17in (44 x 43cm)

WORKING THE DESIGN
The design area is 174 stitches wide and 173 stitches high, excluding the background outside the ribbon. You should extend the background to make the chair seat the desired size, but you will need more of the background color if the seat is bigger than 20in (51cm) square. Using a single strand of tapestry yarn, work the design in tent stitch. The color key gives the main uses of each color. See page 114 for tent-stitch techniques and blocking and finishing instructions.

COLOR KEY
This design was made in Appleton (Ap) tapestry yarn. Alternative yarns listed on page 124 will give a slightly different effect.

Ap 225 – dark rose pink – 2 skeins
some flowers

Ap 755 – mid rose pink – 2 skeins
some flowers and some flower centers

Ap 753 – light rose pink – 2 skeins
some flowers

Ap 706 – pastel pink – 2 skeins
some flowers and some flower centers

Ap 125 – terracotta – 2 skeins
some flower centers, leaves, and stems

Ap 695 – dark gold – 2 skeins
yellow rose and some flower centers

Ap 471 – light yellow – 2 skeins
yellow rose and some flower centers

Ap 851 – cream – 9 skeins
background only

Ap 881 – off-white – 2 skeins
some flowers and leaf veins

Ap 242 – dark olive green – 2 skeins
leaves and stems

Ap 343 – mid gray-green – 2 skeins
leaves and stems

Ap 542 – light green – 2 skeins
leaves and stems

Ap 646 – dark blue-green – 1 skein
some leaf veins and flower centers

Ap 853 – dark blue – 2 skeins
ribbon and blue flowers

Ap 322 – mid blue – 3 skeins
ribbon and blue flowers

Ap 152 – light blue – 3 skeins
ribbon and blue flowers

Ap 151 – pale gray-blue – 2 skeins
leaves only

Ap 603 – mid lilac – 1 skein
some flowers

Ap 601 – light lilac – 1 skein
some flowers

FORGET-ME-NOT TEAPOT

The robust 18th-century writer Samuel Johnson speaks of "a hardened and shameless tea drinker, who has for twenty years diluted his meals with only the infusion of this fascinating plant; whose kettle has scarcely time to cool; who with tea amuses the evening, with tea solaces the midnight, and with tea welcomes the morning."

Not for Johnson the elegance of the drawing-room tea party! But the very idea and ritual of "sitting down to a cup of tea" is such a lovely way of sharing a moment with a friend, that I have designed a whimsical cushion and tea cozy as a tribute to this English obsession.

Against the light jade body of my "tea pot," I have swirled ivy, which represents fidelity, for it clings to one's dwelling; everlasting love, for it is evergreen; and tenderness, for it does not harm that to which it is attached. I have added pansies for kind thoughts; rich purple violets for faithfulness; sky-blue forget-me-nots for remembrance; and a stripy tulip for its sheer painterly effect.

I chose bay (the sacred "laurel" of the ancients, with which poets and victors were crowned) for the border of the cushion. It was believed to ward off the lightning that "cleaves things asunder," and couples would wear a sprig to demonstrate their constancy. I added gold threads for a dash of classical elegance, and a dragonfly resting on the lid of the teapot to help you lift it!

*L*ove and scandal are the best sweeteners of tea.

LOVE IN SEVERAL MASQUES,
HENRY FIELDING
(1707–1754)

The Forget-me-not Teapot tea cozy with its candy-striped, twisted handle (left), and a detail from the 17th-century FLORILEGIUM *by Johann Walther (above)*

71

MAKING THE CUSHION OR COZY

MATERIALS

• Appleton tapestry yarn in 12 colors and Twilley's *Goldfingering* (metallic thread) in gold
• 10-mesh ecru double-thread canvas 20 x 18in (51 x 46cm) for cushion or cozy
• Size 18 tapestry needle
• ½yd (50cm) of fabric for backing and matching sewing thread for cushion or cozy
• 12in (30cm) zipper for cushion
• 1½yd (1.4m) of ready-made cord for cushion or 1½yd (1.4m) for cozy
• Four 4in (10cm) tassels for cushion
• Pillow form slightly larger than needlepoint (or padding for tea cozy)
Design size: 14 x 12in (36 x 30.5cm)

Detail from THE DUKE OF PENTHIEVRE AND HIS FAMILY *(below), by Louis Michel van Loo (1707–1771)*

WORKING THE DESIGN

The chart is 140 stitches wide and 121 stitches high. Using a single strand of tapestry yarn, or two strands of gold metallic thread, work the design in tent stitch. The color key gives the main uses of each color. See page 120 for finishing instructions for tea cozy.

COLOR KEY

This design was made in Appleton (Ap) tapestry yarn. Alternative yarns listed on page 124 will give a slightly different effect.

Ap 944 – rose pink – 6 skeins
center background

Ap 473 – mid yellow – 1 skein
border shading and flowers

Ap 471 – light yellow – 2 skeins
border and flowers

Ap 254 – dark olive green – 3 skeins
teapot leaves and border leaves

Ap 544 – light olive green – 1 skein
background dots and border leaves

Ap 432 – jade green – 15 skeins
teapot background

Ap 463 – mid blue – 1 skein
forget-me-nots

Ap 803 – light fuchsia – 1 skein
pansy and violet centers, and tulip

Ap 454 – violet – 1 skein
teapot flowers

Ap 893 – light lilac – 1 skein
teapot flowers

Ap 895 – dark lilac – 1 skein
line border and teapot patterns

Ap 881 – off-white – 1 skein
teapot handle, spout, and flowers

gold metallic thread – 1 ball
dragonfly wings and teapot details

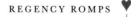

ROMANTIC LONGINGS

*L*ove for the Victorians was romantic, sentimental, and nostalgic. Domestic virtues were exalted, and the home was seen as a refuge of moral and spiritual values in the new Industrial Age. Women, their bodies encumbered by corsets, crinolines, and bustles, read novels in serial form, played the piano, taught the Scriptures in Sunday schools, pressed flowers, and stitched.

Lily of the Valley cushion (left), and a typically romantic Victorian "scrap," probably originally an embellishment on an early valentine

Under their young Queen, and after almost a century of constricting good taste, the new Victorians in Britain gave free rein to their emotions, if not to their desires. Popular literature, poetry, architecture, and painting all showed a romantic nostalgia for the past, and soon the delights of the Gothic were to be joined by those of Arthurian romance.

The Industrial Revolution had brought wealth to Britain; it had also brought exploita-

THE AWAKENING OF ADONIS *(right), by John William Waterhouse (1849–1917), and a cupid detail from* LAUS VENERIS *(below), by Sir Edward Burne-Jones (1833–1898)*

---

*G*ot up at 20m to 9. My dearest Albert put on my stockings for me. I went in and saw him shave; a great delight.

QUEEN VICTORIA'S JOURNAL,
FEBRUARY 13TH, 1840

---

tion, social unrest, and a revival of religious fervor aimed at the poor. Romantic and sentimental yearnings were the prerogative of the better-off, who closed their eyes (and their curtains) to the poverty and prostitution outside, and filled their houses with all the paraphernalia of wealth: heavy and upholstered furniture, fire screens, revivalist plaster-work and stained glass, berlin work, and love seats.

The home was a shelter from the anxieties of modern life where the longings of the soul could be realized, a refuge for moral and spiritual values. Painters, poets, and novelists often portrayed childhood as a blessed time and the home was lit by the light of a pastoral imagination.

However, social conscience and artistic integrity at times went hand in hand. Toward the end of the century, William Morris and the Pre-Raphaelites embraced both Socialism and the craft-based values of the Middle Ages. Turning their back on the materialism of mass production, they created their own domestic ideal, in which individualism, artistic skills, human emotions, and sexuality were always encouraged to flourish.

The Pre-Raphaelites turned to nature as inspiration, adorning their works with the care of the medieval illuminator. Imbued though they were with the romance of Arthurian England, Morris's designs, with their overblown acanthus, lilies, pomegranates, and roses in somber shades, quickly provided a new and influential artistic inspiration. The skilled craftsmanship of the Pre-Raphaelites pervaded all layers of crafts, including printing, weaving, embroidery, and tile-making. They strove to raise the status of every laborer to craftsman and demonstrate that absolute beauty was always their goal.

A thing of beauty is a joy forever:
Its loveliness increases;
it will never
Pass into nothingness; but still will keep
A bower quiet for us, and a sleep
Full of sweet dreams, and health,
and quiet breathing.
Therefore, on every morrow,
are we wreathing
A flowery band to bind us to the earth...

ENDYMION, JOHN KEATS (1795–1821)

SNAKE IN THE APPLE TREE

My home is in a very beautiful part of England, where according to legend, Arthurian heroes lived happily after death. In the Vale of Avalon, as it is known, I am surrounded by fields filled in spring with a haze of pink and white apple blossom blowing in the breeze. In autumn, gleaming apples hang on the trees, and a smell of cidery fermentation hovers in the air. When I stand in an orchard, with the great arches of branches over my head, I feel as if I were in a great cathedral.

The apple blossom represents beauty and goodness; it falls, too, like countless tears for a lost love. The apple stands for prosperity and fecundity, as its shape, when cut in half, is suggestive of the female sexual organs. It is appropriate then that this is the symbol of Venus, goddess of love. The Romans believed that if you ate an apple, strength and well-being would be with you.

The coiled circles of the sinuous snake represent the constant regeneration of life, and its eggs symbolize rebirth and fertility. It can also be treacherous, as the Bible tells us in Genesis. The snake seduced Eve with the apple of knowledge, and Eve in turn tempted Adam with her experience. The Garden of Eden was lost for ever, and man was exiled into the cold cruel world. Woman was thereafter blamed for her powers to seduce, enchant and corrupt the innocence of man, and thus her powerful sexuality would always be a double-edged sword. A reworking perhaps of the original Greek legend of Pandora's box.

My design is taken from a William de Morgan tile dating from the end of the nineteenth century. A Pre-Raphaelite potter, de Morgan was an artist-craftsman much influenced by medieval ornament: fruit trees, fantastical creatures, stylized fish, dragons, sunflowers, and peacocks were carefully and patiently applied to his tiles and vases. His palate of green, blue, turquoise, and bull's blood red derived from his love of Turkish Islamic work.

The border for the design comes from another de Morgan piece—a beautiful ceramic vase decorated with fish swimming in a sea of tonal blue. The waves seemed the perfect complement for the main picture, continuing the naturalistic swirls and vivid colors that were the hallmark of de Morgan.

With its sinuous serpent slithering through the branches, leaves, and untouched apples, the Snake in the Apple Tree conveys the our yearning for a Paradise lost.

Snake in the Apple Tree (left), and a detail from EVE AND THE SNAKE *(right), by Lucas Cranach (1472–1553)*

> *Though I am old with wandering*
> *Through hollow lands*
> *and hilly lands,*
> *I will find out where she has gone,*
> *And kiss her lips and take her hands;*
> *And walk among long dappled grass,*
> *And pluck till time and times are done*
> *The silver apples of the moon,*
> *The golden apples of the sun.*
>
> THE SONG OF WANDERING AENGUS,
> WILLIAM BUTLER YEATS (1865–1939)

MAKING THE HANGING

MATERIALS

• Appleton tapestry yarn in 12 colors
• 10-mesh ecru double-thread canvas 15 x 31in (39 x 78cm)
• Size 18 tapestry needle
• ½yd (50cm) of fabric for backing and matching sewing thread
• 2¼yd (2.3m) of olive green ready-made cord for edging and 8in (20cm) of turquoise cord for top loop
• Two 4in (10cm) olive green tassels to hang from two bottom corners
• Piece of strong cardboard
Design size: 10 x 25½in (25.5 x 65cm)

WORKING THE DESIGN

The chart is 100 stitches wide and 255 stitches high. Turn the chart so that it is the right way up, and using a single strand of tapestry yarn, work the design in tent stitch. The color key gives the main uses of each color. See page 116 for tent-stitch techniques and page 121 for finishing instructions.

COLOR KEY

This design was made in Appleton (Ap) tapestry yarn. Alternative yarns listed on page 124 will give a slightly different effect.

Ap 205 – light terracotta – 3 skeins
urn, inner border, and apples

Ap 842 – gold – 2 skeins
apples and snake stripes

Ap 337 – dark olive green – 2 skeins
snake only

Ap 333 – light olive green – 6 skeins
border background and leaves

*Detail of the hanging and of a
ceramic tile designed by
William de Morgan (below)*

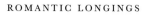

 Ap 294 – dark green – 2 skeins
apple tree branches and leaf veins

Ap 355 – light green – 3 skeins
leaves

Ap 642 – light gray-green – 3 skeins
urn pattern and leaves

Ap 831 – jade green – 1 skein
snake's eye and spine

Ap 526 – dark aqua – 4 skeins
apple tree and urn outlines

Ap 482 – turquoise – 6 skeins
center background

Ap 567 – dark sky blue – 4 skeins
dots, border swirls, and urn pattern

Ap 324 – mid gray-blue – 4 skeins
border swirls and urn pattern

VICTORIAN FLOWERED HEART

Flowers have been used as symbols of love and friendship since earliest times, but the Language of Flowers was elevated to an art form in the Victorian period.

There is a need in every one of us to express our emotions: a request for kindness, a cry from the heart, an amorous suggestion. At times we are too shy to speak our heart, or feelings run too deep for words. At those times a posy or an embroidered token can express what we cannot utter: a simple declaration of love, an apology, a celebration of an anniversary, a declaration of a grand passion!

My Victorian Heart cushion is composed of spring and summer flowers—a Victorian herbaceous border ablaze with bright blues, pinks, and purples counterbalanced with softer tones of yellow and cream. The background of duck-egg blue throws forward the lush blooms while two ruffled

Victorian Flowered Heart cushion (right), surrounded by summer roses, and a Victorian butterfly "scrap" (above)

*T*hrough sunny May,
    through sultry June,
I loved her with a love eternal;
I spoke her praises to the moon,
I wrote them to the Sunday Journal:
My mother laughed; —I soon found out
That ancient ladies have no feeling;
My father frowned; —but how should gout
See any happiness in kneeling?

WINTHROP MACKWORTH PRAED (1831)

*S*he's my myrtle, my geranium,
    My sun flower,
    my sweet marjoram.
My honey suckle, my tulip, my violet,
My holly hock, my dahlia, my mignonette.

THE BROKEN-HEARTED GARDENER, ANON.

wired ribbons and a twisted cord add a Victorian flourish.

In the Language of Flowers, my green leafy border promises only the lightest of involvements, and a hint that the blossoms of love may fade. Seize the moment! Make hay while the sun shines!

There are roses, of course; they represent divine love and Christian virtue, as well as human love—anything from a deep attachment to passionate carnal attraction. Cabbage roses are the messengers of love, and rosebuds indicate young love and the "sweet thoughts that will dwell forever in your bosom."

The daisy, one of the earliest flowers of spring, represents simple innocence; the pansy kind thoughts and happy memories; violets are for faithfulness; primroses suggest birth (and always remind me of plump babies' bottoms); the lily of the valley indicates the return of happiness; morning glory, affection; cornflowers, delicacy; and forget-me-nots sprinkled everywhere are for remembrance. And of course, there is also the butterfly, which represents an old love renewed.

My loving posy is tied with a white polka-dot blue bow; the color blue always declares the depth of true love.

MAKING THE CUSHION

MATERIALS

• Appleton tapestry yarn in 19 colors
• 10-mesh ecru double-thread canvas 22 x 21in (56 x 52cm)
• Size 18 tapestry needle
• ½yd (50cm) of fabric for backing, sewing thread, and 14in (36cm) zipper
• 1½yd (1.4m) ready-made cord
• One 3in (7.5cm) gray-green tassel
• 3m (3¼yd) of two colors of wired ribbon
• Pillow form slightly larger than design
Design size: 16 x 14½in (40.5 x 37cm)

WORKING THE DESIGN

The chart is 160 stitches wide and 146 stitches high. Mount the canvas on an embroidery frame. Using a single strand of tapestry yarn, work the design in tent stitch. The color key gives the main uses of each color. Note that shade 881 (oyster) is also used for bow dots, morning glory centers, and one of the butterflies. The forget-me-not flower centers are worked in 862 or 473, the white daisy centers in 473 and the violet centers in 862 and 473. See page 114 for technical tips.

A heart-shaped Victorian valentine, adorned with ruffles (above)

COLOR KEY

This design was made in Appleton (Ap) tapestry yarn. Alternative yarns listed on page 124 will give a slightly different effect.

Ap 947 – dark raspberry – 1 skein
flower centers and roses

Ap 945 – mid pink – 1 skein
roses, morning glories, and ribbon

Ap 754 – pastel pink – 2 skeins
roses

Ap 703 – pale pink – 1 skein
roses and lily of the valley

Ap 881– white – 2 skeins
white flowers and roses, etc.

Ap 767 – brown – 1 skein
leaf veins and leaf outlines

Ap 862 – orange – 1 skein
yellow flower centers and butterflies

Ap 473 – mid gold – 1 skein
yellow flowers and violets

Ap 551 – light yellow – 2 skeins
butterflies and yellow flowers

Ap 158 – dark blue-green – 1 skein
violet dots, leaves, and butterflies

Ap 156 – mid blue-green – 2 skeins
leaves

Ap 254 – dark olive green – 2 skeins
leaves and stems

Ap 543 – light olive green – 2 skeins
leaves and stems

Ap 351 – pale gray-green – 1 skein
some white flowers and roses

Ap 521 – pale blue – 6 skeins
background

Ap 822 – dark blue – 1 skein
blue flowers and bow

Ap 463 – light blue – 3 skeins
blue flowers and bow

Ap 455 – dark violet – 1 skein
violets

Ap 885 – light violet – 1 skein
violets

CHERUBS

My Cherubs cushion includes all the ingredients needed for a declaration of true love. Three little cherubs hold aloft a rich red heart encircled by azure blue forget-me-nots. Purple violets mean loving thoughts, roses indicate unwavering love, and the blue ribbon carries the message, in Latin, "Love Through Friendship." To crown it all, a pair of doves signifying marital bliss and devotion are set against a sky of swirling gray and salmon-colored clouds. It was believed that birds chose their mates on Valentine's Day so it was sometimes called Birds' Wedding Day.

Valentine's Day was originally the pagan fertility festival of Lupercalia, held in mid February to celebrate the arrival of spring and a young man's fancy. Later, the Christian Church adopted the festival, naming it after one of their saints, St Valentine, who died for his faith on 14th February.

The Victorians really adopted the day with fervor, using it as an opportunity to renew vows of love or declare their feelings for a sweetheart.

Tokens of love had existed in one form or another for centuries, but now they were made into works of magpie ornamentation. Perforated paper, lace, silk flowers, ribbons, ruffles, embroidered and embossed card were all used for these confections, which were then hand-colored. I made my Cherubs cushion in the spirit of these sentimental tokens of undying love.

Detail from CUPID'S KISS *(above), by E. M. Munier (c. 1895), and two Cherubs cushions, in a swathe of spring cherry blossom (right)*

MAKING THE CUSHION

A typically sentimental Victorian valentine, complete with violets and scantily clad cherubs (above)

MATERIALS
• Appleton tapestry yarn in 19 colors
• 10-mesh ecru double-thread canvas 22 x 23in (56 x 57cm)
• Size 18 tapestry needle
• ½yd (50cm) of fabric for backing and matching sewing thread
• 14in (35cm) zipper
• 2yd (1.8m) of ready-made cord for edging
• Pillow form slightly larger than finished needlepoint design
Design size: 16 x 16¹/₂ in (41 x 42cm)

WORKING THE DESIGN
The chart is 160 stitches wide and 165 stitches high. Using a single strand of tapestry yarn, work the design in tent stitch. The color key gives the main uses of each color. Note that shade 987 (off-white) aside from being used for the doves and the cherubs' wings is also used for the tiny white flowers and for a few parts in the clouds. The flower centers are worked in 695 (light gold). See page 114 for tent-stitch techniques, blocking and finishing instructions, and technical tips.

COLOR KEY
This design was made in Appleton (Ap) tapestry yarn. Alternatives listed on page 124 will give a slightly different effect.

Ap 227 – dark raspberry – 3 skeins
ribbon, heart, and flower

Ap 757 – light raspberry – 3 skeins
ribbon, heart, flower, and mouths

Ap 125 – dark terracotta – 1 skein
cherubs

Ap 204 – mid terracotta – 4 skeins
cherubs and clouds

Ap 121 – light terracotta – 4 skeins
cherubs and clouds

Ap 696 – dark gold – 1 skein
letters, cherubs' hair, and some flowers

Ap 695 – light gold – 1 skein
letters, cherubs' hair, and some flowers

Ap 355 – dark green – 1 skein
leaves and stems

Ap 401 – light green – 1 skein
leaves and stems

Ap 152 – pastel gray-blue – 4 skeins
doves, clouds, and cherubs' wings

Ap 929 – dark blue – 3 skeins
ribbon, cherubs' eyes, and clouds

Ap 747 – mid blue – 3 skeins
ribbon and clouds

Ap 746 – light blue – 3 skeins
ribbon, clouds, and dove's collar

Ap 821 – pale blue – 1 skein
blue flowers only

Ap 455 – dark violet – 1 skein
some flowers

Ap 102 – light violet – 1 skein
some flowers

Ap 976 – dark brown – 2 skeins
cherubs' hair, doves' beaks, and clouds

Ap 965 – gray – 3 skeins
clouds

Ap 987 – off-white – 2 skeins
doves, cherubs' wings, etc.

LILY OF THE VALLEY

The fragrant Lily of the Vale,
So elegantly fair,
Whose sweets perfume the fanning gale,
To Chloe I compare

ANON. (C. 1780)

The delicious scent of lily of the valley always evokes memories of my American childhood: sweet days visiting elderly relations, and walking down through a grove of pine trees to a lake. Under the trees, masses of the delicate white pearls nestled among their large, curving leaves; it was like the Garden of Eden.

Lily of the valley flowers speak of a return to happiness or maidenly modesty: "Friendship is precious; talk to me not of love." Like the open mouths of birds on a fragile stem,

Lily of the Valley needlepoint cushion (right), and a detail from THE WEDDING MEAL *(below), by Albert-August Fourie (b. 1854)*

the small white bells are sometimes called Our Lady's Tears, and were said to grow where the Virgin Mary's tears fell.

A friend, knowing my compulsive hoarding of odds and ends of all kinds, gave me a book of Victorian scraps. In it were cuttings and collages of childhood: rural images, hands holding cards, nosegays, birds, angels with butterfly wings, baskets of violets—and a basket of lily of the valley. It was this whole mood of nostalgia and forgotten innocence that I was keen to capture in this softly feminine design.

I used various tones of white for the flowers, greens for the leaves, and ochers for the golden wicker. The bluey-lilac background is complementary to the yellows and throws the delicate design forward. And since this was a tribute to Victorian sentimentality, the lace border was a must for creating a period feel.

I made the cushion as a token of love for my grandmother, whose favorite flower (and scent) was lily of the valley. You, too, may have a special person for whom you can make this needlepoint.

I feel sad when I don't see you. Be
married, why won't you? And
come to live with me. I will make you as
happy as I can. You shall not be obliged to
work hard; and when you are tired, you
may lie in my lap and I will sing you to
rest…Will you be married?

19TH-CENTURY AMERICAN LOVE LETTER

MAKING THE CUSHION

MATERIALS
- Appleton tapestry yarn in 13 colors
- 10-mesh ecru double-thread canvas 20 x 20in (51 x 51cm)
- Size 18 tapestry needle
- ½yd (50cm) of fabric for backing and matching sewing thread
- 12in (30cm) zipper
- 2¼yd (2m) each of gold and of light-green ready-made cord for double-cord edging
- Four 2½in (6.5cm) gold tassels
- Pillow form slightly larger than design

Design size: 14 x 14in (35.5 x 35.5cm)

WORKING THE DESIGN
The chart is 140 stitches wide and 140 stitches high. Using a single strand of tapestry yarn, work the design in tent stitch. The color key gives the main uses of each color. Note that if you want to edge the cushion with a single ready-made cord, you will need only 1¾yd (1.6m) of cord. See page 114 for tent stitch techniques, blocking and finishing instructions, and technical tips.

COLOR KEY
This design was made in Appleton (Ap) tapestry yarn. Alternative yarns listed on page 124 will give a slightly different effect.

Ap 222 – mid rose pink – 1 skein
ribbon

Ap 707 – light rose pink – 1 skein
ribbon

Ap 767 – brown – 1 skein
basket

Ap 696 – dark gold – 1 skein
basket and handle

Ap 473 – mid gold – 2 skeins
basket and handle

Ap 471 – yellow – 8 skeins
basket, border, and background dots

Ap 841 – cream – 1 skein
flowers only

Ap 294 – dark gray-green – 1 skein
leaves

Ap 832 – mid green – 1 skein
leaves

Ap 402 – light green – 1 skein
leaves

Ap 541 – pale green – 1 skein
leaves

Ap 892 – lilac – 7 skeins
center background

Ap 991 – white – 6 skeins
border pattern and flowers

Detail of the Lily of the Valley needlepoint cushion with its namesake (below)

MODERN PASSION

*M*odern love is sexy, selfish, and cynical. There's no time for courtship. The delicate rose of romance has been withered by two World Wars, and shredded in the tornadoes of emancipation and self-interest. As the blooms are scattered, and the maggot of disappointment and hypocrisy revealed for what it is, we toss up the petals and create our own moral rules and patterns of courtship.

"I Love You" cushion (left), based on a design by British artist Peter Blake, and a detail from HEARTS "A" *by Paul Giovanopoulos (above)*

*S*weet spring is your
time is my time is our
time for springtime is lovetime
and viva sweet love

E. E. Cummings (1894–1962)

This century has seen swiftly changing values, and a revolt against the conventions of previous generations. Women have been the prime movers: they cut their hemlines and their hair, smoked cigarettes, got the vote, bought washing machines and, when it became available, took the pill.

Men, too, reacted to the pressures of mass unemployment after the first and second World Wars and gradually became more alienated as their status as provider was put into question.

Finally, the 1960's witnessed the complete overthrow of traditional values. Sex, drugs, and rock'n'roll were the liberators and the annihilators. Today, the apparent celebration of uninhibited sex gives rise to a sense of urgency, immediacy, intense emotion, and spontaneity. In this mobile and quickly changing world individual self-expression is what is sought. And with the collapse of the social order that supported communities, marriages, and families, we seem to have isolated ourselves and lost our balance—our creative spiritual center.

The "Me Generation" is today in a state of disenchantment. Unlike our forefathers, who could rely on a collective opinion concerning the nature of man and reality, all now is uncertainty; anything goes.

It may be true that we are not as instinctively creative as the pagans, as eloquent as the courtiers, as mannered as the Georgians, or as sweetly optimistic as the Victorians. Yet we too, like the men and women of other generations, other cultures, other times, cannot live without love. As Edward VIII declared in his abdication speech: "I have found it impossible to carry the heavy burden of responsibility and to discharge my duties as King as I would wish to do without the help and support of the woman I love."

Perhaps the high divorce statistics show not failure but a struggle for a new expression of love: an equilibrium in which friend, protector, comforter, confidant, and lover are all rolled into one. We desire a communion of all our senses, and recognize the need to reintroduce a spiritual element into our lives, to become aware of our "soul," to reconnect with nature. The touch of a finger, the glory of music, the full blossom of a chestnut tree, the zaniness of a sea shell are all transforming visions and proof enough that there is love.

We know today how hate can destroy the world; we have no other choice *but* to love.

Nighthawks *(below), by American artist Edward Hopper (1882–1967)*

*T*he pain of
    loving you
Is almost more than
    I can bear.

A YOUNG WIFE,
D. H. LAWRENCE
(1885–1930)

THE GREEN TURBAN *(left),*
by Tamara de Lempicka
(1898–1980)

JAZZY BAG

"Love and work. Work and love. That's all there is…," wrote Sigmund Freud. Gustav Klimt, also from Vienna and a contemporary of Freud, often threaded the eminent psychiatrist's dream world through his work. His themes centered on Eros, the god of love, on the Greek myths, and on life's natural cycle.

To Klimt, women were bearers of life's mysteries, and intimately linked with nature. Danae, a symbol of carnal and sensual loveliness, is the subject of one of Klimt's paintings (below right). She was locked away by her father to prevent her from conceiving a child that the oracle had prophesied would kill him. Zeus fell in love with Danae and visited her secretly as a golden shower of spermatazoa.

Klimt conveys the ecstasy of this union of god and woman, depicting the life-giving stream surging down between Danae's voluptuous thighs. Her wild red hair reminds me of the wavy locks of Botticelli's Venus, another symbol of sexual beauty and divine love.

This painting is just one of the sources for my Klimt interpretation, which, like his own work, is also an amalgam of organic patterns that have no obvious beginning or ending. I wanted to capture the jazzy rhythm, the flood of colors, and wealth of ornament. Klimt's mosaic-like composition of repetitive squares, circles, and spirals in taupes, mustards, purple, coral, and splashes of gold interact to give a painterly effect and a be-bop beat to the needlepoint.

When she rises in the morning
I linger to watch her;
She spreads the bath-cloth
underneath the window
And the sunbeams catch her
Glistening white on the shoulders.
While down her sides the mellow
Golden shadow glows as
She stoops to the sponge,
and her swung breasts
Sway like full-blown yellow
Gloire de Dijon roses.

GLOIRE DE DIJON,
D. H. LAWRENCE (1885–1930)

The coral Jazzy Bag (left), and a detail from DANAE *(below), by Gustav Klimt (1862–1918)*

MAKING THE BAG

MATERIALS
• Appleton tapestry yarn in 11 colors and
Twilley's *Goldfingering* (metallic thread) in gold
• 10-mesh ecru double-thread canvas 18 x
15in (46 x 38cm)
• Size 18 tapestry needle
• Small piece of fabric for lining and match-
ing sewing thread
• 2yd (1.8m) of ready-made cord for strap
and edging
• One 4in (10cm) gold tassel
Design size: 11½ x 8in (29 x 20.5cm)

WORKING THE DESIGN
The chart is 115 stitches wide and 80 stitches
high. Using a single strand of tapestry yarn, or
two strands of gold metallic thread, work the
design in tent stitch. The color key gives the
main uses of each color. See page 114 for the
various tent-stitch techniques and page 118 for
blocking instructions.

One length of cord is used to form the edging
and the strap. After blocking, line the bag and
attach the strap (see page 122).

COLOR KEY
This design was made in Appleton (Ap) tapestry yarn. Alternative yarns listed on page 124
will give a slightly different effect from that
shown in the picture on page 98.

 Ap 208 – maroon – 3 skeins
bottom stripe and some checks

Ap 866 – dark coral – 1 skein
checks and large swirl background

Ap 865 – light coral – 1 skein
large swirl background

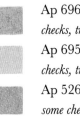 Ap 696 – dark mustard – 2 skeins
checks, triangles, and large swirls

Ap 695 – light mustard – 1 skein
checks, triangles, and large swirls

Ap 526 – aqua – 1 skein
some checks and thin border line

Detail from SALOME *(above),*
a painting by Gustav Klimt
(1862–1918)

 Ap 328 – dark blue – 1 skein
small swirls and some checks

 Ap 456 – violet – 1 skein
some checks and triangles

Ap 894 – lilac – 1 skein
triangles, small circles background, etc.

Ap 975 – taupe – 2 skeins
checks and small swirls background

Ap 881 – white – 1 skein
some checks and triangles

 gold metallic thread – 1 ball
checks, triangles, and large swirls

ICON OF DIVINE LIGHT

Cecil Collins was a British painter much influenced by the redemptive power of nature and preoccupied by the metaphysical world. He said of his work: "My own painting is essentially of the heart." When the Royal Academy in London asked me to choose a piece of this visionary artist's work, who died in 1989, I chose his "Icon of Divine Light" painting. This combines the sacred geometry of the sunflower with the sun's rays, the shining stars of the firmament, and the serene beauty of a woman's face.

*E*verthing that is lovely in nature became illuminated by the thought of her.

LOVE AND DEATH,
LLEWELYN POWYS
(1884–1939)

Collins believed that man was ennobled by his relationship with nature, which fed his interior life. He speaks of "the poetic imagination" and "the creative God in man." Like many earlier mystic visionaries and Romantics such as Samuel Palmer, William Blake, and J. M. W. Turner, Collins saw the divine presence in all things: in a rainstorm, in shafts of sunlight coming through the clouds, in a speck of dust.

In all Collins's work there is a sense of wonder, a reverence for all natural things. The original painting from which my work is done is an altar frontal for a chapel in Chichester Cathedral. It seems to me an affirmation that now is the time for a reawakening of the positive in us. Burnt sienna, golden yellow, and a delicate light cream interact across the canvas to celebrate the glorious resurgence of nature.

Icon of Divine Light needlepoint (right), and FIANCÉS ON A GREEN BACKGROUND *(above), by Marc Chagall (1887–1985)*

MAKING THE CUSHION

MATERIALS
- Appleton tapestry yarn in 6 colors
- 12-mesh white interlock canvas 28 x 18in (71 x 46cm)
- Size 18 tapestry needle
- ½yd (50cm) of fabric for backing and matching sewing thread
- 20in (51cm) zipper
- 3yd (2.8m) of ready-made gold cord (enough for double knots at corners)
- Pillow form slightly larger than design

Design size: 22 x 12in (56 x 30.5cm)

ICON OF DIVINE LIGHT *(below), the altar front in Chichester Cathedral, by Cecil Collins (1908–1989)*

WORKING THE DESIGN
The chart is 264 stitches wide and 144 stitches high. Using a single strand of tapestry yarn, work the design in tent stitch. The color key gives the main uses of each color. Note that it is not necessary to follow the chart exactly when working the random-effect background. See page 114 for tent-stitch techniques and finishing instructions.

COLOR KEY

This design was made in Appleton (Ap) tapestry yarn. Alternative yarns listed on page 124 will give a slightly different effect.

 Ap 954 – brown – 8 skeins
outlines

Ap 696 – dark gold – 2 skeins
sun and sun's rays

Ap 695 – mid gold – 4 skeins
sun and stars

Ap 842 – light gold – 12 skeins
background and sun

Ap 551 – yellow – 9 skeins
background and sun

Ap 841 – cream – 2 skeins
highlights on sun and stars

HOT LIPS

*before leaving my room
i turn,and(stooping
through the morning)kiss
this pillow,dear
where our heads lived and were.*

E. E. CUMMINGS (1894–1962)

What is the origin of the Kiss? For centuries man has puzzled over the attraction of this erogenous zone. Did kissing originate in our desire to taste our loved ones, or in the smacking of lips in anticipation or pleasure? Or did

The Hot Lips cushion (right), and AT THE HOUR OF THE OBSERVATORY, THE LOVERS *(above), by Man Ray (1890–1976)*

it begin with the newborn baby sucking at its mother's breast for warmth and sustenance?

We have a need for our senses to be stimulated, and kissing involves touch, smell, and taste. The lips and the heart symbolize for me the sensory pleasures that love brings. Kissing lips hungrily search for the inner sense of heart and soul. "My own dear boy," wrote Oscar Wilde to Lord Alfred Douglas, "... your sonnet is quite lovely and it is a marvel that those red roseleaf lips of yours should be

made no less for the music of song than for the madness of kissing. Your slim gilt soul walks between passion and poetry."

My Hot Lips cushion is a tribute to the sensual pouts that have kissed the face of 20th-century art. Man Ray's modernist lips, drifting eerily in search of a face to inhabit, suggested the shape for my design. And then there is Andy Warhol's Marilyn (page 111), whose lips scorch through the screenprint and burn desire into eternity. I wanted my Lips to capture the teasing mood of her lipstick pout.

Other design triggers included Dali's pneumatic lip-shaped sofa and Lichtenstein's cartoon-strip embraces. Like all of these, my modern pink Lips are hot, wild, and zany. What a perfect love token!

*Yes when I put the rose in my hair like
the Andalusian girls used
or shall I wear it red yes and how
he kissed me under the Moorish wall and
I thought well as well him as another
and then I asked him with my eyes to ask
again yes and then he asked me would
I yes to say yes my mountain
flower and first I put my arms around him
yes and drew him down to me so he
could feel my breasts all perfume yes
and his heart was going like mad and
yes I said yes I will Yes.*

ULYSSES, JAMES JOYCE (1882–1941)

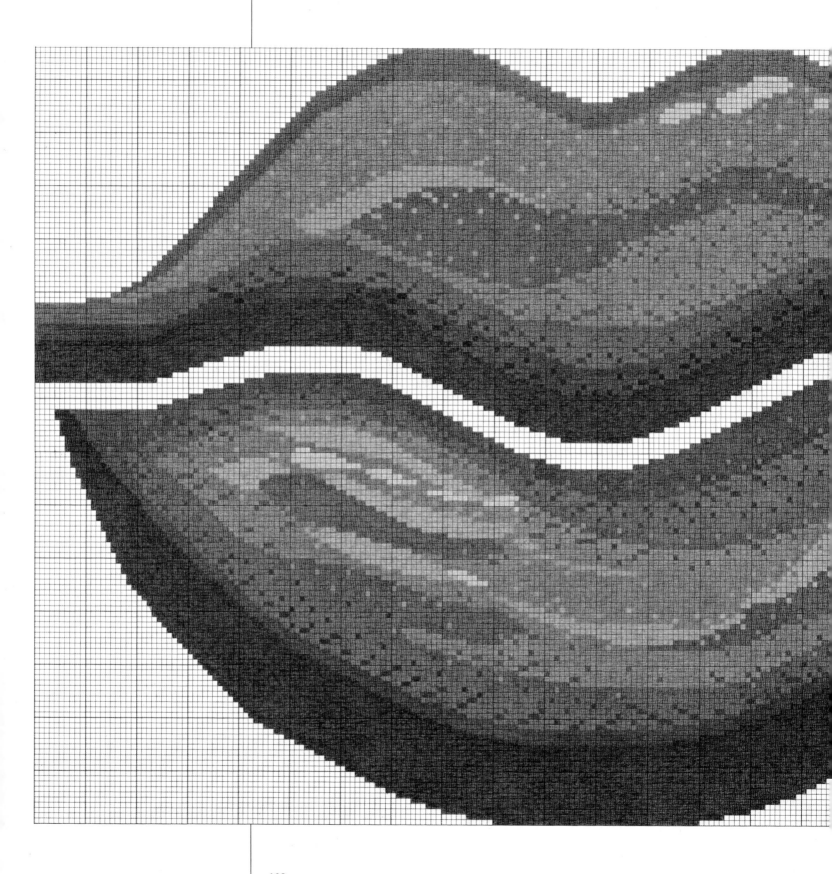

MAKING THE CUSHION

MATERIALS
- Paternayan Persian yarn in 6 colors
- 10-mesh ecru double-thread canvas 24 x 28in (61 x 71cm)
- Size 18 tapestry needle
- ¾yd (70cm) of satin fabric for backing, matching sewing thread and stuffing
- 1.6m (1¾yd) of hot pink ready-made cord

Design size: 14 x 22in (35.5 x 56cm)

WORKING THE DESIGN
Mount the canvas on an embroidery frame to ensure that it retains it will retain its shape. Using two strands of Persian yarn, work the design in tent stitch. Note that the two lips must be worked at least 3in (8cm) apart to allow for seam allowances. See page 119 for finishing instructions.

COLOR KEY
This design was made in Paternayan (Pa) Persian yarn. Alternative yarns listed on page 124 will give a slightly different effect.

Pa 940 – dark red – 10 skeins
lower edge of both lips

Pa 941 – mid red – 7 skeins
shading color

Pa 960 – hot pink – 11 skeins
lip color

Pa 961 – light hot pink – 10 skeins
lip color

Pa 963 – light pink – 1 skein
lip highlights

Pa 353 – fuchsia – 2 skeins
lip highlights

I wasn't kissing her, I was whispering in her mouth.

CHICO MARX (1891–1961)

I LOVE YOU

Peter Blake, painter and collector of the flotsam of urban life, is unique: wholly original in the way he looks at the world, and a master of everything he touches. His love of popular imagery reveals itself in girlie magazines, the circus, Americana, wrestlers, strippers, matinée idols, and pop stars. But he comes from a tradition that paints with affec-

Some say that love's a little boy,
And some say it's a bird.
Some say it makes the world go round,
And some say that's absurd,
And when I asked the man next door,
Who looked as if he knew,
His wife got very cross indeed,
And said it wouldn't do.

O TELL ME THE TRUTH ABOUT LOVE,
W.H. AUDEN (1907–1973)

tion, that feels for the people and the objects that appear on the canvas; his work is intensely personal (as all true art must be), and he realizes it with meticulous and loving care.

Blake frequently adds found objects to his paintings—toys, badges, fragments, flags, romantic postcards, royal memorabilia—yet the effect resulting from his rejoicing in the trivia of life never confuses the strength of the end result. He often adds typographic lettering to enhance his pictures and create the whole scrap-book effect.

Blake's obsession with clutter, using up life's leftovers, is very dear to my own heart. I am renowned for my inability to throw things

away—strands of tinsel, broken china, old postcards all adorn the magpie nest I call home. All these tokens of trivia await the moment when they can be useful again and justify my feverish collecting.

Yet like Blake, I find that these fragments, the jetsam of life, acquire an importance far beyond their surface utility, simply because they have been used, admired, and then just rejected. Sometimes the old and worn is so much more appealing than the "brand new."

"I Love You" is from a series of Blake prints featuring the heart motif and using primary colors to frame it. I was asked by the Royal Academy to translate one of his designs into needlepoint. A seemingly simple task—but it was important to avoid making the colors too flat. I finally managed to resolve this by using two tones of yarn for each main area. This had the effect of enlivening the colors.

The "Scrabble"-like letters spelling out the amorous declaration are divided by lines of gray stitching to suggest Peter's original typographic cardboard squares. Finally, I added matt black cord to dramatize the design and made four chunky corner tassels. Each tassel is wrapped with a main color, adding a playful note to the whole.

The end result of my interpretation of Blake's original is wholly satisfying. The simplicity of this image has great strength—clear vivid colors making a shrine around the bright pink heart, shouting out "I Love You!"

"I Love You" cushion (left), and MARILYN MONROE *screenprint (above), by Andy Warhol (1928–1987)*

MAKING THE CUSHION

Persian yarn, you will need one extra skein of 220 (black) for each tassel. Full instructions for making tassels are given on page 120. See page 114 for the various tent-stitch techniques, blocking and finishing instructions, and technical tips.

COLOR KEY

This design was made in Paternayan (Pa) Persian yarn. Alternative yarns listed on page 124 will give a slightly different effect.

Pa 961 – dark pink – 6 skeins
heart

Pa 962 – light pink – 4 skeins
heart

Pa 820 – dark tangerine – 3 skeins
inner border

Pa 821 – light tangerine – 3 skeins
inner border

Pa 726 – dark yellow – 2 skeins
center background

Pa 760 – bright yellow – 2 skeins
center background

Pa 653 – light olive green – 1 skein
background for letters

Pa 454 – beige – 2 skeins
background for letters

Pa 541 – dark blue – 4 skeins
blue border

Pa 542 – light blue – 4 skeins
blue border

Pa 220 – black – 5 skeins
letters and outer border

Pa 211 – blue-gray – 1 skein
lines between letters only

MATERIALS
• Paternayan Persian yarn in 12 colors
• 10-mesh ecru double-thread canvas 19 x 19in (47 x 47cm)
• Size 18 tapestry needle
• ½yd (50cm) of fabric for backing and matching sewing thread
• 11in (28cm) zipper
• 1½yd (50cm) of ready-made cord
• Four 4in (10cm) black tassels
• Pillow form slightly larger than design
Design size: 12³/₄ x 12³/₄ in (32 x 32cm)

WORKING THE DESIGN
The chart is 127 stitches wide and 127 stitches high. Using three strands of Persian yarn, work the design in tent stitch. The color key gives the main uses of each color. There is no need to follow the chart exactly when working areas of speckled colors as long as the colors are worked in a similar random fashion. Note that if you want to make your own tassels with

NEEDLEPOINT TECHNIQUES

Approaching needlepoint from the perspective of a designer, I was not initially trained in the technical how "and why." Because I was eager to translate my visions quickly into needlepoint and had only just grasped the basic stitch, I jumped right in. Moving arbitrarily from one area of the design to the next, I scrunched up the canvas in my hand and scooped up my stitches in a single movement. Needless to say, the back of my early canvases ended up a real mess, but my delight at seeing my imaginings realized overcame this minor detail!

Though my technique has improved since, I am still impatient for quick results, which means that my way of working may not seem quite "proper" to the more meticulous embroiderer. Hopefully the following simple tips and pointers, which I have picked up along the way, will help you if you are a beginner. But if you know of or find an easier way to work, do not hesitate to use it.

When stitching, try to be patient with yourself, using as much of the technical information as you can without feeling constrained by rules. Do not make your stitching arduous for yourself; instead, work in the way that is the most comfortable and enjoyable for you. In my experience, needlepoint can be so absorbing and fruitful!

NEEDLEPOINT MATERIALS
Needlepoint Yarns
Many different yarns can be used in needlepoint: wool, cotton, linen, silk, rayon, and even metallic threads. In this book I have used mainly Appleton tapestry yarn because of its superb range of colors, and I would strongly encourage you to order it through Appleton's mail-order suppliers (see page 125) if you fail to get it locally. However, if you do prefer to use another brand of yarn, turn to the color conversion chart on page 124 that lists equivalent shades for three of the main yarn manufacturers.

Yarn colors vary from brand to brand, so if you do use an alternative yarn, the finished result will not match my original design exactly and will give a slightly different effect. But when preparing the conversion chart, I have tried to keep the shades in tune with the spirit of my originals.

Wool needlepoint yarn most commonly comes in three different weights—crewel, Persian yarn, and tapestry. Tapestry yarn is the thickest, and crewel the finest. The aim in choosing the correct yarn for your work is to select one that will adequately cover the canvas.

A single strand of tapestry yarn is fine for a 10- or 12-mesh canvas. Persian yarn comes in three strands which are easily separated; two or three strands are required for a 10-mesh canvas, and two for a 12-mesh canvas. Crewel yarn is only slightly finer than Persian. Four strands of crewel yarn should cover a 10-mesh canvas and three strands a 12-mesh.

For my Renaissance Heart pincushion (page 46), I have used a rayon thread (see page 127), which I chose for its jewel-like quality. Unfortunately it is slippery to work with and can become tangled, so it may not be a good choice for the beginner or the impatient. As an alternative, I have suggested that you use cotton embroidery thread because it is easier to use and has a luminous quality much like the rayon.

On my Renaissance Heart I have also used *Madeira* gold thread, which adds an antique flavor to the design. The gold metallic thread used on the purses (pages 14, 42, and 98) and on the Florentine Angel and Venus's Robe cushions (pages 34 and 38) is washable and will not tarnish. These golden touches on my designs can be worked in any suitable metallic embroidery thread, or crochet or knitting yarn. If you do use a brand different from the one I have specified, you will have to experiment with how many strands to use on the 10-mesh canvas.

Canvas
There are three different types of needlepoint canvas to choose from—mono (or single-thread), interlock, and double-thread (or Penelope). My preferred canvas is ecru double-thread canvas. I find a double-thread canvas more convenient as it allows me to work any of the tent stitch techniques. An ecru double-thread canvas is also easier to draw on and the result-

ing lines are clearer. But, *most importantly*, if any canvas does show through your finished stitches, the ecru color is less harsh and obvious than a glaring white.

When I do use a mono canvas, it is for a specific reason. For instance, for the Georgian vest (page 54) I needed a soft canvas and smaller stitch details, so I chose a 12-mesh interlock canvas. Beginners might find mono canvas better, as double-thread canvas can be confusing. Mainly I suggest that you use what you can find.

Embroidery Frames

One of the beauties and luxuries of needlepoint for me is that I can carry it around; for that reason alone, I usually do not use a frame. I am quite hard on my work, rolling and folding it, taking it here, there, and everywhere—on planes and trains, outside in the garden or at the beach, and in waiting rooms. But because my tension is even and not too tight, and because I stretch my canvases afterward, all turns out brilliantly flat! If you stitch with a tighter tension, this haphazard way of working may not suit your needs. In this case, you should stretch your work on an embroidery frame.

For vests or other shaped designs, like my Renaissance Heart pincushion or my Greek Urn cushion, I did use a frame. I would strongly advise you to use a frame for any needlepoint like these that is other than square or rectangular. The frame ensures that the work retains its shape and, when finished, does not require excessive blocking (see page 118).

NEEDLEPOINT STITCHES
Before Beginning

Before you begin your needlepoint, make sure that you will be working in a comfortable situation with good light. Anyone involved professionally in the fine or decorative arts will tell you that the most important element in your working conditions is good light. One item I highly recommend (and wonder how I ever lived without) is a daylight simulation light bulb. It is essential for working at night and I even use mine during the day. If you have not used one, I beg you to try one; close colors will never baffle you again! These bulbs can be found in art supply, household, and electrical stores.

Working from a Chart

The advantage of working needlepoint from a chart is being able to see your plain canvas develop as your design grows. Also, you avoid the confusion that you may sometimes encounter on a printed canvas, where a color falls between two holes. Those of you who do prefer working tent stitch on a printed canvas, however, will be pleased to find that many of the designs featured in this book are available as kits (see page 125 for kit information).

When working from a chart, note that each square on the graph equals one stitch on your canvas. You simply count the number of squares of a particular color on the chart, then work this number of stitches onto the canvas.

If the chart is split across two pages in the book and you find this difficult to read, you could have a color photocopy made of each page and then tape the two copies together. Also, if the squares are too small for you to read with ease, have a color enlargement made or use a magnifier or a magnifying strip.

Preparing the Canvas

You should always allow 2in to 3in (5cm to 8cm) of extra canvas all around the needlepoint design. This is later trimmed when the backing is sewn on. Before beginning your needlepoint, it is a good idea to fold masking tape over the raw edges of the canvas. This stops the canvas from unraveling and insures that your yarn will not catch on rough edges.

If you are working from a chart, begin by marking the outside dimensions of the whole design on the canvas with a brightly colored thread or a permanent ink pen (never use a pencil as it soils the work). For another point of reference, you could also run colored threads through the center of the canvas, vertically and horizontally.

Make a paper template of the design area at this stage, so that you have a size guide to use later for blocking the finished needlepoint.

It is usually better to work the various motifs in a design first, leaving the background until last. You can either work from the center outward, or from the upper left-hand corner diagonally downward so that you are not rubbing over areas already worked.

Tent Stitch

Because I am interested in the color and design of needlepoint first and foremost, rather than in the stitches used, I only work with the most familiar basic stitch known as "tent stitch." This stitch can be worked in three different ways—the simple half-cross technique, the continental technique, and the basket-weave technique.

The right side of the embroidery looks the same with all three techniques, but the appearance of the back of the work varies. Each method has its advantages and disadvantages, so use whichever you are used to or, if you are a beginner, try all three and use whichever you are most comfortable with. You can use different techniques on the same canvas, but when filling in large areas in a solid color, such as backgrounds or large single-color motifs, try to use one technique or you may create visible ridges on the front of the work.

Threading your Needle

One thing I am quite definite about is the length of yarn one should use when working tent stitch – between 14in and 18in (35cm and 45cm). If the yarn is used in lengths which are too long, it gets twisted and also frays and becomes thinner toward the end of the strand, especially with the darker colors. When you start your needlepoint, measure a 16in (40cm) length of yarn only once, just to get a feel for the correct length. Thereafter you will be able to judge automatically how long to cut the strands.

Always use a tapestry needle, which has a blunt point; a needle with a sharp point would split the wool yarns and the needlepoint canvas. The eye of the tapestry needle must be big enough to accommodate the thickness of the yarn easily, but not so thick that you have to force it through the canvas. I suggest you use a No. 18 needle for all the designs in this book, which are worked on either 10- or 12-mesh canvas.

When threading your needle, run your fingers over the tapestry yarn in one direction, then the other. The thread will feel smoother in one direction and the yarn should be threaded so that it is inserted and pulled through the needlepoint canvas in the "smooth" direction. This is not essential, but it does help prevent the yarn from fraying.

Beginning your Stitching

Detailed instructions for how to work the three different tent-stitch techniques are given on the following pages, but the method of starting and finishing the ends of the yarn is the same for each of the techniques.

To start, knot the end of the yarn. Then, about 1in (2.5cm) from where you want to start, insert the tapestry needle through the needlepoint canvas from the right side to the wrong side. Pull the yarn through, leaving the knot on the front surface. As stitching progresses, the yarn end underneath will be secured by the stitches worked over it.

When the length of yarn is finished, secure the end by running the needle through a line of stitches at the back. Alternatively, you can bring the yarn back to the front 1in (2.5cm) away from the last stitch, leaving it to be secured underneath with more overlapping stitching. The knots and loose ends on the surface of the work should be snipped away carefully as they are secured.

When you re-thread the needle to continue in the same area, there is no need to knot the yarn: simply run the needle and yarn through a few stitches at the back, and bring the yarn to the front in the correct position. When doing this, avoid bringing the needle up through a hole already partially filled with yarn, as needles can split the thread. Try to work down into partially filled holes in order to smooth the yarn. If you have to unpick any mistakes, use small pointed scissors, being careful not to cut the canvas inadvertently.

One thing to remember about your stitch tension is that it is wise to work darker backgrounds a bit looser so that they cover the needlepoint canvas entirely. Darker colored yarns tend to be slightly thinner than lighter colored yarns due to the effect of the dyes.

Half-cross Stitch

The half-cross technique for working tent stitch is the easiest of the three techniques and uses the least amount of yarn. Because it forms short vertical stitches on the back, which do not entirely cover the back of the canvas, the resulting embroidery is not as thick as a needlepoint worked in either of the other two tent-stitch techniques. It is ideal for filling in just a few isolated stitches in a particular color; but if used on a large area of a solid color, the needlepoint canvas may distort. This technique should be worked on a double-thread or interlock needlepoint canvas.

Continental Tent Stitch

Continental tent stitch can be worked on any type of canvas. It forms a firmer fabric than the half-cross stitch and the back of the work is entirely covered with yarn.

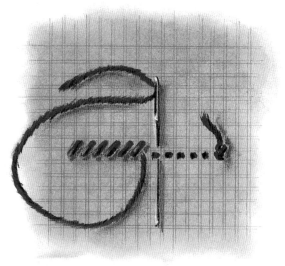

When beginning your stitching, work over the loose end at the back of the work as described on page 116. Cross the yarn over each intersection of the double canvas threads, making short stitches at the back.

When beginning, work over the loose end at the back of the canvas as described on page 116. Work the first row of stitches from right to left as shown, making diagonal stitches at the back.

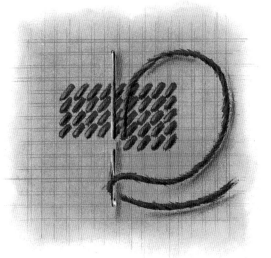

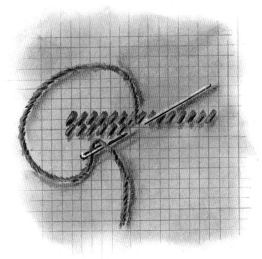

Work the rows of stitches from left to right and from right to left alternately, with the needle pointed alternately upward and downward with each row as shown. If you find it easier to always work from left to right, you can turn the canvas after each row.

Work the next row of stitches above or below the first, but moving in the opposite direction. If you are working without a frame and using only one hand to make the stitches, you can to turn the canvas upside down after each row so that you are always working from right to left if desired.

Basketweave Tent Stitch

Basketweave tent stitch is worked in diagonal rows. It is good for covering large areas of background. The resulting needlepoint is very stable and will not distort. This stitch can be worked on any type of canvas.

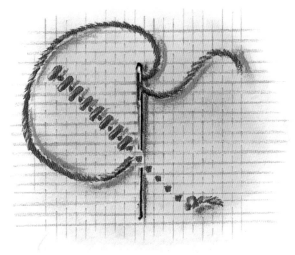

At the beginning, work over the loose end as described on page 116. Work the first row diagonally downward from left to right as shown, forming vertical stitches at the back of the canvas.

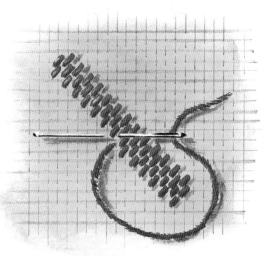

Work the next basketweave tent stitch row diagonally upward, forming horizontal stitches at the back of the needlepoint canvas as shown in the illustration above. Work all the following basketweave tent stitch rows downward and upward alternately.

FINISHING YOUR NEEDLEPOINT
Blocking

If you have worked your needlepoint with the canvas stretched very tautly in an embroidered frame, it may not need blocking, which entails stretching and dampening. But if you have worked it in the hand, it will definitely need to be smoothed out and may even need to be pulled vigorously into shape.

If you find that the task of stretching seems a bit daunting, ask a friend for help. You may even prefer to have your needlepoint stretched and backed professionally. Your local furnishing fabric store or art supply store may be able to help.

If you are blocking your work at home, you will need a clean board on which to stretch the needlepoint and, of course, rust-proof tacks and a hammer. I use steel-tempered thumb tacks instead of ordinary tacks, which I find easier to use (see page 126 for supplier). Needlepoint canvas is very strong, so you can pull quite hard when stretching the finished work. Wool yarns, especially, are amenable to being stretched.

Place the finished canvas face down on the board. Spray the back with a fine mist of water or dampen it with a sponge. Then stretch the canvas into shape, nailing into the raw canvas as you stretch. Begin with a tack at the center of each of the four sides, then work outward from the center, placing the tacks about 1in (2.5cm) apart. Allow the needlepoint to dry completely before removing it from the board; this may take a whole day. After blocking, back or line the needlepoint immediately.

Backing a Cushion

Choose the color of your backing fabric to enhance or complement your needlepoint. Before beginning to back the work, trim the canvas to within ¾in (2cm) of the tent stitches.

The easiest way to insert a zipper into your cushion backing is to position it in a center seam. In this case, you should cut two pieces of fabric of equal size, allowing a ¾in (2cm) seam allowance around all sides. Use your blocked needlepoint to determine the size of the backing.

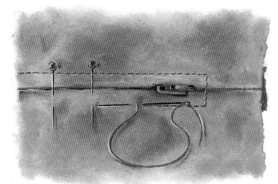

Begin by joining each end of the center seam, leaving an opening for the zipper. Then pin the zipper to the wrong side and sew in place using a sewing machine with a zipper foot or working by hand in backstitch.

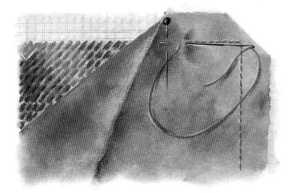

Press the completed center seam, then pin the backing to the needlepoint with the right sides together. Using backstitch or a sewing machine, stitch all around the needlepoint, leaving a gap the width of one tent stitch between the edge of the embroidery and the seam. Leave a small opening at one corner for inserting the cord ends. Clip the corners of the seam allowance diagonally, and turn right side out. The narrow band of raw canvas around the edge of the work will be covered later by the cord.

Backing a Shaped Cushion

A shaped cushion is backed in the same way as an ordinary cushion. So for the Greek Urn and the Victorian Heart (pages 18 and 22), begin by cutting two pieces of backing fabric that, once sewn together up the center, will be large enough to form a rectangle covering the back of the finished needlepoint, with 1in (2.5cm) extra all around the outer edge. Insert the zipper in the center seam and press the backing. Trim the backing to the same size and shape as the blocked and trimmed needlepoint, allowing for a ¾in (2cm) seam.

Next pin the backing to the needlepoint, with the right sides together. Stitch around the edge of the needlepoint as for an ordinary cushion. Before turning right side out, clip the seam allowance along the seam to ease the curves.

If you do not wish to insert a zipper in your backing, you can merely leave an opening by overlapping two pieces of backing by 4in to 5in (10cm to 13cm) across the center. This type of opening is especially suitable for shaped cushions.

Cushion Pads for Shaped Designs

For shaped cushions you will need to make your own cushion pads in the shape of the design. One important thing to remember is that shaped cushions need to be stuffed very firmly to best show off their shape.

The Hot Lips cushion (page 106) is finished off in a way that enhances the sculptural shape of the lips. It does not have a removable pillow form.

After blocking and trimming the needlepoints, cut two pieces of backing fabric the same size as the two trimmed lips including a ¾in (2cm) seam allowance. Then pin the upper and lower needlepoint lips together along the center and sew tightly so that no canvas is showing. Turn the remaining raw canvas edges to the wrong side and pin in place. (If you are using covered piping, sew it to the needlepoint edge at this stage.)

Press the seam allowances on the two backing pieces to the wrong side and pin one to each needlepoint lip. Sew the backing pieces to the needlepoint by hand, oversewing along the center and along the outside edges, leaving a small opening on the outside edge of each lip for stuffing. Stuff the lips firmly and close the openings, leaving a small gap for the cord ends.

Attaching Cords and Ribbons

It is best to take your finished—but as yet unblocked—needlepoint with you when you are choosing the ready-made cord or braid. Pick one that enhances the design.

Before cutting your cord always wrap tape around it close to where you are going to cut it. This is essential as it will stop the cord from unraveling.

When sewing on the cord, place it over the seam between the needlepoint and the backing (or lining) and push the ends into the small opening that has been left in one of the corners of the seam (see illustration above). To add a decorative touch I often form loops, knots, or twists with the cord at the corners of the needlepoint.

On the Victorian Heart (page 82), I used wired ribbon as well as ready-made cord for the trimming. Two shades of ordinary ribbon could be substituted for the two shades of wired ribbon on this heart-shaped cushion, but wired ribbon is especially easy to use. The wire on the inner edge of the ribbon can be pulled to gather it into a ruffle; the wire on the outer edge keeps the ruffle crisp.

Making Tassels

Tassels can be purchased ready-made and vary in price. However, you can make your own tassels quite easily and the advantage of this is that they can be any color you wish and can be made out of any thread. Be generous when calculating the amount of yarn or thread you will need for your tassels, as thick tassels look better than skimpy ones.

Wrap the chosen thread many times around a piece of cardboard which is slightly longer than the desired length of the finished tassel. With a separate length of thread, tie the strands together at one end of the piece of cardboard, leaving long loose ends. Then cut the strands along the other end of the cardboard.

Make a loop at one end of a long piece of thread and place it so that the looped end is about 1¼ in (3cm) below the top of the tassel, with the cut end extending upward. Wrap the other end tightly around and around the top of the tassel as shown. Then slip the end of the thread through the loop and pull both ends of the thread in order to pull the final end under the thread wrappings. Cut off the loose ends and trim the end of the tassel.

MAKING A TEA COZY

The Forget-me-not Teapot design (page 70) can be made into a cushion or a tea cozy. To make a tea cozy, first cut a piece of backing fabric the same size as the blocked and trimmed needlepoint – which includes a ¾in (2cm) seam allowance.

For the lining, cut two more pieces the same size and shape as the back. Then cut two pieces of thick padding the same shape as the lining but omitting the ¾in (2cm) seam allowance all around the edge.

Sew the needlepoint to the back with the right sides facing, leaving the bottom edge open and leaving a small opening at the top for a cord loop. Clip along the seam to ease the curves. Do not turn right side out.

Sew the two lining pieces together in the same way. Turn under the lower edge of the tea cozy and baste in place. Place one piece of padding on the wrong side of the needlepoint and one piece on the wrong side of the cozy back. Slip the lining over the padding and stitch it to the cozy along the lower edge and the center seam, leaving a small opening at the lower edge of one seam.

Turn the cozy right side out and sew a cord loop into the small center top opening. Then sew cord along the center seam and along the lower edge tucking the cord ends into the opening at the bottom of the seam.

MAKING A HANGING OR PICTURE

To mount the Snake in the Apple Tree hanging (page 78) you will need a large piece of strong cardboard. After blocking do not trim the unworked canvas, but leave the extra 3in (7.5cm) all around the stitching.

Stretching over cardboard

Cut a piece of cardboard a fraction of an inch (centimeter) larger all around than the size of the embroidered area.

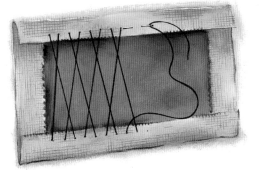

Lay the needlepoint face down and place the cardboard on top of it . Then fold the long canvas edges to the back over the cardboard. Using a very strong thread, lace the sides together as shown, pulling tightly. Lace the remaining ends together in the same way.

Backing the hanging

Cut a piece of backing fabric the same size as the stretched design, plus a ¾in (2cm) seam allowance all around. Sew a loop of cord to the back of the needlepoint at the center top. Turn under the seam allowance on the backing and stitch it to the needlepoint, covering the lacings and leaving a small opening in one corner.

Sew the cord around the edge, tucking the ends into the corner opening. Then sew a tassel to each of the lower corners.

The Medieval Cornflower picture (page 42) can be mounted on cardboard in the same way before framing, but you should get advice from your framer first.

MAKING A PINCUSHION

After blocking the Renaissance Heart needlepoint pincushion (page 46), leave at least 2in (5cm) of raw canvas all along the edge. Sew on the beads as desired. Cut a piece of backing fabric the same size as the embroidered area, plus a ¾in (2cm) seam allowance and set aside.

Stretching over cardboard

Cut two pieces of strong cardboard the same size and shape as the embroidered area and two or three layers of padding the same size and shape as the cardboard pieces.

Lay the needlepoint face down and place the layers of padding, then one piece of heart-shaped cardboard on top of it. Lace the canvas edges together over the cardboard (see Making a Hanging above), pulling tightly. There will be unworked canvas around the edges, but this will be covered later by the braid or ribbon trimming.

Place the second piece of heart-shaped cardboard over the laced back. Then turn under the seam allowance all around the edge of the backing and sew it to the back of the pincushion, covering the cardboard.

Attaching trimming

Sew braid or ribbon around the edge of the heart so that it butts up to the embroidery, covers the raw canvas edge and overlaps the backing. Sew the bobbles to the braid and sew the tassel to the point of the heart.

MAKING A PURSE OR BAG

Needlepoint purses and bags such as the Egyptian Eye purse, the Medieval Cornflower purse, and the Jazzy bag (pages 14, 42, and 98) are very easy to finish. After the needlepoint has been completed, block and trim as usual (page 118).

Lining and Backing the Purses

The Egyptian Eye and Medieval Cornflower purses are both lined and backed in the same way. You should first cut two pieces of lining fabric and one piece of backing fabric, all the same size as the trimmed needlepoint including a ¾in (2cm) seam allowance. Turn under the raw canvas edges on the needlepoint and the seam allowance on one piece of lining and sew the two pieces together with the wrong sides facing. Sew the second piece of lining to the back of the purse in the same way, leaving a small opening in the top two corners for tucking in the cord ends. Then sew the lined back to the lined front.

Lining the Jazzy Bag

To line the Jazzy bag, first cut a piece of fabric the same size as the trimmed needlepoint allowing for a ¾in (2cm) seam.

Join the side seam of the bag from top to bottom. Press the seam open and turn right side out. Then turn under the raw canvas along the lower edge and using a strong thread gather the edge tightly, closing the bottom of the bag. Make the lining into the bag shape in the same way and insert it into the bag.

Turn under the top edges of the lining and the bag and sew together, leaving a small opening at the seam and another on the opposite side to tuck in the cord ends.

Attaching straps

Cord is used to trim the purses and bag and to form the long straps. On the Egyptian Eye and Medieval Cornflower purses, sew the cord along the top edge of the needlepoint, then along the remaining three edges, ending at the top edge. Leave a long, loose length of cord for the strap and stitch the cord ends into the openings left at the top of the purse. On the Jazzy bag, sew the cord all around the top edge of the needlepoint, then make the strap and insert the cord ends in the gaps left on opposite sides of the top edge.

MAKING A VEST

If you are not an accomplished sewer, be sure to seek help when sewing together your needlepoint vest. The embroidery will have taken you a great deal of time and effort and it would not be wise to risk damaging it. You might even prefer to have a local seamstress back and line the vest for you, which is what I did.

If you do decide to sew the vest together yourself, you will find that lining the needlepoint fronts of the vest designs is done in much the same way as a backing is made for a shaped cushion, with the finished fronts serving as the templates for cutting the front lining. The pattern for the back of the Georgian vest (page 54) is given here.

Before beginning the back, block your needlepoint and trim the raw canvas to within ¾in (2cm) of the stitching. Trace the shapes of the trimmed fronts on pattern paper and cut out. These paper pieces will be used later for making the lining.

Sewing on the Back

Begin by drawing one half of the vest back on a piece of pattern paper marked with 1in (2.5cm) squares. Use the diagram as your guide. Then, for the seam allowance, draw a line all around the outline ¾in (2cm) from the edge. Cut out the pattern piece.

Fold the fabric for the back so that the fold runs with the grain of the fabric. Place the pattern piece on the fabric, lining it up with the grain of the fabric, and pin in place. Cut along the edge of the paper pattern and remove the pins. Note: If you are in doubt about the accuracy of your paper pattern, it is best to test it first with an inexpensive fabric remnant.

Cut two pieces of fabric 8½in by 3in (22cm by 8cm) for the back belt. Fold each piece in half lengthwise with the right sides facing. Stitch across one short end and along the long side ½in (1.5cm) from the edge. Turn the two belt pieces right side out and press. Sew in the dart on each half of the back, inserting the end of one belt piece in each dart seam about 4in (10cm) above the lower edge.

Join the center back seam. Then with right sides facing, pin the shoulders of the vest back to the shoulders of the trimmed needlepoint fronts and stitch together close to the needlepoint.

GEORGIAN VEST BACK

Note: Each square measures 1in (2.5cm) x 1in (2.5cm). Measurements given are finished measurements and do not include seam allowances.

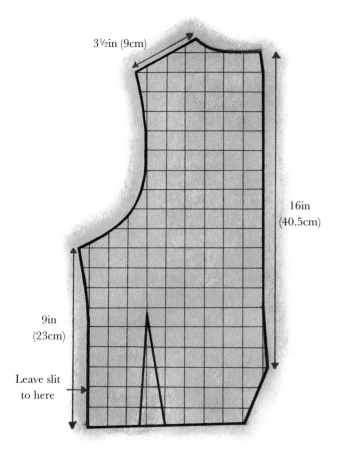

3½in (9cm)

16in (40.5cm)

9in (23cm)

Leave slit to here

Join the side seams in the same way, but leaving the lower edges open to allow for a 1¾in (4.5cm) finished slit. Press open all of the seams on the wrong side of the vest.

Making the Lining

Before lining the vest, turn under the raw canvas along the right center front edge and sew three cord button loops to the vest. Position the first loop level with the armhole, the second 7½in (19cm) below the first, and the third half way between the first two.

Using the paper pattern, cut two back pieces and two fronts from the lining fabric. Sew the backs together, then sew the back and front linings together in the same way the back was sewn to the needlepoint fronts. Trim and press the seams.

Sewing on the Lining

With the right sides together, pin the lining to the vest around the front edges and neck only. Machine stitch the pieces together along this edge close to the embroidery. Where necessary clip the curved edges of the seam just made. Turn right side out and press.

Turn the seam allowance to the wrong side around the armholes of the lining and the vest. Sew the lining to the vest all along the armholes by hand.

In the same way as for the armholes, turn under the seam along the lower edge of the lining and the vest, making a slit at each side seam. Sew the lining to the vest along the lower edge (including the slit) by hand and press.

Finishing the Vest

If necessary, fill in any empty canvas along the edges of the needlepoint with tent stitch. Then sew the ready-made cord along the front, neck, and lower edges of the embroidery. Sew the buttons to the wrong side of the left front edge and sew the buckle to one end of the belt.

NEEDLEPOINT CHAIR SEATS

Although covering a chair seat with needlepoint may take a long time because it is bigger than an ordinary cushion, it is well worth the effort. My Aubusson Roses chair seat on page 66 can be made to fit any size seat by extending the background. If you want to make this design into a chair seat, you will first have to make a template of the correct size for your chair. Some shops that offer the service of sewing the finished needlepoint to chair seats will also make you a template. The template outline is then drawn on the canvas before the stitching is begun. After the needlepoint has been completed, the canvas should be stretched and blocked to match the template.

CLEANING YOUR NEEDLEPOINT

A wool needlepoint will not require very frequent cleaning. If you do need to clean it, however, it is best to have it dry cleaned. Be sure to take it to a reputable dry cleaner and, if there is any metallic thread in the embroidery, follow the manufacturer's dry cleaning advice.

YARN CONVERSION CHART

The following color conversion chart is provided for readers who wish to use an alternative wool yarn. All of the Appleton (and Paternayan) shades used in the book are listed here, and each shade is followed by the closest equivalent available in Paternayan (or Appleton), DMC, and Anchor yarns. These alternatives, however, are only approximate equivalents and will therefore give a slightly different effect from that shown in the pictures. Appleton tapestry yarn comes in 11yd (10m) skeins. If you buy an alternative yarn that comes in a smaller skein, be sure to allow for this. The alternative yarns are also "tapestry"-weight wool except for Paternayan Persian yarn, which consists of three strands. When using Persian yarn and working tent stitch on a 10-mesh canvas, use two or three strands; for a 12-mesh canvas use only two strands.

Cotton embroidery thread equivalents are also given here as the alternative for Anchor Marlitt rayon threads used on the Renaissance Heart (page 46).

Note: The yarn amounts given in the instructions are for continental and basketweave tent stitch (see pages 117 and 118). You will need about 20 per cent less yarn if the needlepoint is worked entirely in half-cross stitch (see page 116).

WOOL YARNS

Ap = Appleton tapestry yarn – 11yd (10m) per skein
Pa = Paterna Persian yarn – 8yd (7.4m) per skein
DMC = DMC Laine Colbert – 8¼yd (8m) per skein
An = Anchor tapestry yarn – 11yd (10m) per skein

RAYON AND COTTON THREADS

Mt = Anchor Marlitt Viscose Rayon – 11yd (10m) per skein
DMC = DMC no. 5 pearl cotton – 11yd (10m) per skein
An = Anchor no. 5 pearl cotton – 11yd (10m) per skein

APPLETON TAPESTRY (first four columns) · **PATERNA PERSIAN** (last four columns)

Ap	Pa	DMC	An	Ap	Pa	DMC	An	Ap	Pa	DMC	An	Ap	Pa	DMC	An	Pa	Ap	DMC	An
102	312	7709	8590	358	601	7379	9208	696	731	7780	8102	872	715	7905	8012	211	924	7593	8718
121	486	7543	9596	401	613	7424	9258	703	947	7121	8296	881	263	blanc	8002	220	993	noir	9800
125	481	7840	9600	402	612	7384	9018	706	875	7121	8296	885	302	7709	8588	353	801	7153	8488
149	900	7115	8426	432	687	7545	8984	707	874	7122	8344	892	343	8604	7711	454	341	7371	9056
151	203	7331	9064	454	301	7708	8526	721	871	7356	9560	893	342	7711	8606	541	823	7796	8692
152	534	7692	8894	455	300	7708	8592	722	860	7446	9562	894	342	7711	8608	542	464	7797	8690
154	534	7323	8876	456	300	7242	8530	726	860	7184	8264	895	340	7243	8610	653	251A	7373	9304
155	533	7326	8880	463	543	7798	8688	745	560	7796	8644	903	740	7477	9406	726	553	7435	8120
156	532	7701	8882	464	542	7317	8690	746	502	7317	8630	929	571	7307	8742	760	997	7433	8116
158	531	7329	8884	471	727	7727	8566	747	500	7318	8794	934	320	7119	8428	820	445	7606	8196
204	485	7123	8326	472	726	7726	8058	753	923	7193	8396	935	421	7372	9684	821	443	7946	8194
205	872	7146	8328	473	726	7785	8022	754	905	7194	8414	944	904	7135	8416	940	948	7137	8442
208	870	7447	8242	478	720	7401	9540	755	932	7759	8400	945	903	7135	8438	941	995	7108	8440
222	873	7951	8346	482	583	7807	8806	757	902	7207	8402	947	902	7640	8442	960	947	7600	8456
225	930	7758	8402	521	515	7322	8874	761	454	7724	9482	948	901	7138	8442	961	946	7603	8454
226	901	7147	8404	525	522	7956	8918	764	435	7455	9446	954	440	7487	9330	962	945	7804	8454
227	900	7218	8404	526	521	7596	8922	765	413	7508	9448	965	201	7626	9794	963	943	7605	8452
242	651	7363	9216	541	605	7424	9256	766	412	7457	8064	967	200	7622	9764				
244	651	7355	9310	542	653	7424	9258	767	401	7459	9496	973	462	7275	9370				
254	692	7988	9168	543	693	7770	9166	803	350	8492	7157	974	462	7275	9658				
294	601	7396	9080	544	693	7548	9164	821	543	7316	8644	975	451	7416	9332				
314	651	7573	9288	551	773	7471	8112	822	542	7797	8690	976	450	7416	9662				
322	513	7593	8790	567	580	7318	8674	823	541	7797	8692	987	204	7300	9772				
324	512	7592	8836	568	540	7306	8794	825	540	7820	8692	991	260	blanc	8006				
328	530	7289	8840	588	420	7535	9666	831	662	7542	8968	992	263	ecru	8006				
333	643	7363	9306	601	313	7264	8544	832	661	7909	8970	993	220	noir	9800				
337	640	7471	9332	603	312	7241	8548	841	764	7905	8012	998	221	7624	9798				
342	643	7373	9306	623	833	7875	8234	842	742	7472	8018								
343	643	7362	9260	642	604	7703	9076	851	735	7503	8054								
351	605	7400	9058	646	660	7389	9026	853	501	7591	8794								
354	603	7384	9174	691	654	7501	9322	862	854	7873	9556								
355	602	7376	9176	693	753	7472	8040	865	831	7850	8238								
356	601	7427	9178	694	733	7473	8042	866	850	7920	8236								
				695	732	7506	8100	871	263	blanc	8006								

RAYON THREAD

Mt	DMC	An
1211	3685	44
1209	221	42
881	335	28
830	899	27
1019	3326	24
1079	561	306
1146	367	216
836	824	132
835	826	131
1009	813	130
859	550	101
858	552	100
857	553	98

RETAILERS' ADDRESSES

Kits from Ehrman

Many Candace Bahouth designs are available as Ehrman needlepoint kits. Contact your nearest Ehrman kit retailer or distributor (see Ordering Kits below) for information on the full range of Bahouth designs that can be purchased as kits, many of which do not appear in this book. The Candace Bahouth designs that are featured in this book and are available as kits from Ehrman are as follows:

page 22:	Roman Head cushion
page 38:	Venus's Robe cushion
page 42:	Medieval Cornflower purse
page 54:	Georgian vest
page 60:	Toile de Jouy Cupids cushion
page 66:	Aubusson Roses chair seat
page 70:	Forget-me-not Teapot cushion
page 90:	Lily of the Valley cushion
page 78:	Snake in the Apple Tree hanging
page 86:	Cherubs cushion
page 98:	Jazzy bag
page 102:	Icon of Divine Light cushion
page 110:	"I Love You" cushion

Ordering Kits

To order needlepoint kits contact one of the following kit retailers or distributors:

U.S.A.: EHRMAN, 5 Northern Boulevard, Amherst, New Hampshire 03031. Tel: (800) 433 7899.

U.K.: EHRMAN (shop), 14-16 Lancer Square, Kensington Church Street, London W8 4EP, England. Tel: (0171) 937 8123.

Canada: POINTERS, 1017 Mount Pleasant Road, Toronto, Ontario M4P 2MI. Tel: (416) 322 9461.

Australia: TAPESTRY ROSE, PO Box 366, Canterbury 3126. Tel: (3) 818 6022.

New Zealand: QUALITY HANDCRAFTS, PO Box 1486, Auckland. Tel: (09) 411 8645.

Argentina: VICKIMPORT SA, 25 de Mayo 596, Sp (1002) Buenos Aires. Tel: 322 4247.

Belgium and Holland: HEDERA, Diestsestraat 172, 3000 Leuven. Tel: 016 235997.

Denmark: DESIGNER GARN, Vesterbro 33A, DK 9000 Aalborg. Tel: 9813 4824.

Finland: NOVITA, PO Box 59, 00211 Helsinki. Tel: 358 067 3176.

France: ARMADA, Collange, Lournand, Cluny 71250. Tel: 85 59 1356.

Germany: OFFERTA VERSAND, Bruneckerstrasse 2a, D–6080 Gross-Gerau. Tel: 06152 56964.

Iceland: STORKURINN, Kjorgardi, Laugavegi 159, 101 Reykjavik. Tel: 01 18258.

Italy: SYBILLA, D & C Spa Divisione Sybilla, Via Nannetti, 40069 Zola Predosa. Tel: 051 750 875.

Spain: CANVAS AND TAPESTRY, Costanilla de los Angelez 2, 28013 Madrid.

Sweden: WINCENT, Svearvagen 94, 113 50 Stockholm. Tel: 8673 7060.

Switzerland: BOPP INTERIEUR AG, Poststrasse 1, CH–8001 Zurich. Tel: 1 211 6203.

Needlepoint Yarns

All but three of the designs in this book were worked in Appleton tapestry yarn; of the remaining, two were worked in Paternayan Persian yarn and one in Anchor Marlitt rayon. If you wish to use an alternative brand, see the Yarn Conversion Chart on the opposite page.

Appleton, Paternayan, DMC, and Anchor wool needlepoint yarns are all widely available in needlework shops and department stores. To find a retailer near you, see below or contact the yarn companies or their overseas distributors.

Appleton Mail Order in U.S.A.

See page 126 for advice on finding mail order sources.

Appleton Retailers in U.S.A.

Appleton yarn is available in many retail outlets throughout the U.S.A. The following are a few selected retailers and distributors:

Alabama:

PATCHES & STITCHES, 817A Regal Drive, Huntsville, Alabama 35801. Tel: (205) 533 3886.

SALLY S. BOOM, Wildwood Studio, PO Box 303, Montrose, Alabama 36559. Tel: (334) 928 1415.

California:

FLEUR DE PARIS, 5835 Washington Boulevard, Culver City, California 90230. Tel: (213) 857 0704.

HANDCRAFT FROM EUROPE, 1201-A Bridgeway, Sausalito, California 94965. Tel: (415) 332 1633. Fax: (415) 334 5074.

NATALIE, 144 North Larchmont Boulevard, Los Angeles, California 90004-3705. Tel: (213) 462 2433.

NEEDLEPOINT INC, 251 Post Street, 2nd Floor, San Francisco, California 94108. Tel: (415) 392 1622.

ROSE COTTAGE, 209 Richmond Street, El Segundo, California 90245. Tel: (310) 322 8512. Fax: (310) 322 0187. (See also Mail Order Needlepoint Yarns on following page.)

Delaware:

THE JOLLY NEEDLEWOMAN, 5810 Kennett Pike, Centreville, Delaware 19807. Tel: (302) 658 9585.

Louisiana:

NEEDLE ARTS STUDIO, 115 Metairie Road, Metairie, Louisiana 70005. Tel: (504) 832 3050.

Maryland:

THE ELEGANT NEEDLE LTD, 7945 MacArthur Boulevard, Suite 203, Cabin John, Maryland 20818. Tel: (301) 320 0066.

Massachusetts:

STITCHES OF THE PAST, 68 Park Street, Andover, Massachusetts 01810. Tel: (508) 475 3968. Fax: (508) 683 3146.

Missouri:

SIGN OF THE ARROW–1867 FOUNDATION INC, 9740 Clayton Road, St Louis, Missouri 63124. Tel: (314) 994 0606.

Ohio:

LOUISE'S NEEDLEWORK, 45 North High Street, Dublin, Ohio 43017. Tel: (614) 792 3505.

Pennsylvania:

EWE AND I, 24 North Merion Avenue, Bryn Mawr, Pennsylvania 19010. Tel: (610) 525 3028.

Texas:

ACCESS COMMODITIES (L. HAIDAR), PO Box 1778, Rockwall, Texas 75087. Tel: (214) 722 1211. Fax: (214) 722 1302.

CHAPARRAL, 3701 West Alabama, Suite 370, Houston, Texas 77027. Tel: (713) 621 7562.

DAN'S FIFTH AVENUE, 1520 Fifth Avenue, Canyon, Texas 79015. Tel: (806) 655 3355.

Appleton Retailers in Canada

DICK AND JANE, 2352 West 41st Avenue, Vancouver, British Columbia V6M 2A4. Tel: (604) 738 3574.

FANCYWORKS, 110-3960 Quadra Street, Victoria, British Columbia V8X 4A3. Tel: (604) 727 2765.

JET HANDCRAFT STUDIO LTD, PO Box 91103, 225 17th Street, West Vancouver, British Columbia V7V 3N3. Tel: (604) 922 8820.

ONE STITCH AT A TIME, Thistledown, 78 Main Street, PO Box 114, Picton, Ontario K0K 2T0. Tel: (613) 476 2453.

POINTER INC, 1017 Mount Pleasant Road, Toronto, Ontario M4P 2M1. Tel: (416) 322 9461. Fax: (416) 488 8802.

Appleton Retailers in Australia
CLIFTON H JOSEPH & SON (AUSTRALIA) PTY LTD, 391-393 Little Lonsdale Street, Melbourne, Victoria 3000. Tel: (03) 602 1222.
STADIA HANDCRAFTS, 85 Elizabeth Street, PO Box 495, Paddington, New South Wales 2021. Tel: (02) 328 7973. Fax: (02) 326 1768.
P L STONEWALL & CO PTY LTD (FLAG DIVISION), 52 Erskine Street, Sydney.

Appleton Retailers in New Zealand
NANCY'S EMBROIDERY LTD, 326 Tinakori Road, PO Box 245, Thorndon, Wellington. Tel: (04) 473 4047.

Appleton Main Office in U.K.
APPLETON BROS LTD, Thames Works, Church Street, Chiswick, London W4 2PE, England. Tel: (0181) 994 0711. Fax: (0181) 995 6609.

Appleton Retailers in U.K.
Appleton yarn is available in many retail outlets throughout the U.K., including some branches of John Lewis.
The following are just a few selected U.K. retailers that carry the full range of Appleton tapestry yarn:
London: CREATIVITY, 45 New Oxford Street, London WC1A 1BH. Tel: (0171) 240 2945. Fax: (0171) 240 6030.
W.H.I. LTD, 85 Pimlico Road, London SW1 W8PH. Tel: (0171) 730 5366.
Wiltshire: MACE & NAIRN, 89 Crane Street, Salisbury, Wiltshire SP1 2PY. Tel: (0172) 233 6903.
West Yorksire: THE SPINNING JENNY, Bradley, Keighley, West Yorkshire BD20 9DD. Tel: (01535) 632 469.
Scotland: MISS CHRISTINE RILEY, 53 Barclay Street, Stonehaven, Kincardineshire AB3 2AR. Tel: (01569) 632 38.

Anchor
U.S.A.: COATS AND CLARK, Susan Bates Inc, 30 Patewood Drive, Greenville, South Carolina 29615. Tel: 1 800 241 5997.
Canada: COATS PATONS CANADA, 1001 Roselawn Avenue, Toronto, Ontario M6B 1B8.

Tel: (416) 782 4481. Toll free: 1 800 268 3620. Fax: (416) 785 1370.
Australia: COATS PATONS CRAFTS, 89-91 Peters Avenue, Mulgrave, Victoria 3170. Tel: (03) 561 2288. Fax: (03) 561 2298.
New Zealand: COATS ENZED CRAFTS, East Tamaki, Auckland. Tel: (09) 274 0116. Fax: (09) 274 0584.
U.K.: COATS PATONS CRAFTS, McMullen Road, Darlington, County Durham DL1 1YQ, England. Tel: (01325) 36 54 57. Fax: (01325) 38 23 00.

DMC
U.S.A.: DMC CORPORATION, Building 10, Port Kearny, South Kearny, New Jersey 07032. Tel: (201) 589 0606. Fax: (201) 589 8931.
Canada: See U.S.A.
Australia: DMC NEEDLECRAFT PTY LTD, 51-55 Carrington Road, Marrickville, NSW 2204 or PO Box 317, Earlswood, NSW 2206. Tel: (02) 559 3088. Fax: (02) 559 5338.
U.K.: DMC CREATIVE WORLD LTD, Pullman Road, Wigston, Leicestershire LE18 2DY, England. Tel: (0116) 281 1040. Fax: (0116) 281 3592.

Paternayan
U.S.A.: PATERNAYAN, JCA Inc, 35 Scales Lane, Townsend, Massachusetts 01469. Tel: (508) 597 8794.
Australia: STADIA HANDCRAFTS, 85 Elizabeth Street (PO Box 495), Paddington, New South Wales 2021. Tel: (02) 328 7973. Fax: (02) 326 1768.
Canada: See U.S.A.
New Zealand: THE STITCHING CO LTD, PO 74-269 Market Road, Auckland. Tel: (09) 366 6080. Fax: (09) 366 6040.
U.K.: PATERNA LTD, PO Box 1, Ossett, West Yorkshire WF5 9SA, England. Tel: (01924) 81 19 04. Fax: (01924) 81 08 18

Mail Order Needlepoint Yarns
Specific yarn companies may give advice on how to purchase yarns by mail order, but you can also find out about mail order sevices in the small ads in needlecraft magazines.
The following stores carry the complete range of Appleton tapestry yarn and provide a mail order service as well:

U.S.: ROSE COTTAGE, 209 Richmond Street, El Segundo, California 90245. Tel: (310) 322 8512. Fax: (310) 322 0187.
U.K.: LENHAM NEEDLECRAFT, Heath Lodge, Shurlock Row, Near Reading, RG10 OQE, England. Tel: (01734) 343 207.

Cords and Tassels
A wide range of cords and tassels can be found in stores that sell furnishing fabrics.

Gold, Rayon and Cotton Threads
Cotton, rayon and metallic threads can be found in shops and department stores that sell knitting, crochet, or embroidery threads. The following threads have been used in various designs in this book or have been suggested in the Yarn Conversion Chart on page 124.
Anchor no. 5 pearl cotton (100% cotton)
DMC no. 5 pearl cotton (100% cotton)
Anchor Marlitt Viscose Rayon (100% viscose)
Madeira Metallic Effect Yarn (60% metal and 40% polyester – washable)
Twilley's Goldfingering (20% metallized polyester and 80% viscose – washable)
If you are using an alternative for any one of these threads, experiment on a piece of scrap canvas to decide how many strands of the alternative thread you will need for working tent stitch.

Beads
Beads can be found in specialist bead shops, and the craft or needlework departments of large stores.

Stretching and Backing
Instead of using tacks when stretching and blocking finished needlepoints, I use Assa steel-tempered "drawing pins." These pins have a flat disc-shaped top much like an ordinary thumb tack, but instead of having a single pin on the underside they have three short, strong prongs; they are especially easy to press into wood and to remove. They are often used for stretching silk fabric for silk painting and are available in the U.K. from: GEORGE WEIL AND SONS LTD, 18 Hanson Street, London W1P 7D8, England. Tel: (0171) 580 3763.

If you wish to have your needlepoint stretched and backed professionally, enquire at your local furnishing-fabric or needlework shop to see if they offer this service.

ACKNOWLEDGEMENTS

Without the time and expertise that my "stitchers" have given me, this book couldn't have been "born"—so a grateful thank you to Julia de Salis, Vicki Paton, Vicky Viner, and especially John and Kerri Buxton.

Thank you also—

For the invaluable kindness of Sally and Richard Dennis, Michael and Hillye Cansdale, and Michael and Kate Dunwell, for the use of their very special period homes.

For their support and guidance: Brandon Mabley, Kaffe Fassett, Jeremy Cooper, and Hugh Ehrman.

For the patient, first-rate editing: Louise Simpson, Sally Harding, Caroline Taylor, and John Fletcher.

To the friendly and enthusiastic team at Conran Octopus: Rachel, Tessa, Jane, Eilidh, Suzannah, and "Honey."

To Colin Salmon for his unequaled charts, to Sue Storey and Linda Burgess for the superb visual impact and treats of this book.

To Kathleen Milne for her sewing, to Charlotte Humpston and Lindsay Clarke for the use of their old books, and Titania Hardie for her medieval expertise. And I especially wish to express my appreciation to family and friends who have been so tolerant and given so generously in their own personal ways.

BIBLIOGRAPHY

The Book of Love Symbols. London: Pavilion, 1994.

BECK, Thomasina. *The Embroiderer's Flowers.* David and Charles, 1992.

FIELD, Rachael. *Victoriana.* London: MacDonald Orbis, 1988.

HOUGHTON, Walter E. *Victorian Frame of Mind, 1830–1870.* Yale University Press, 1957.

GRIGSON, Geoffrey, ed. *Faber Book of Love Poems.* London: Faber and Faber, 1973.

HUNT, Morton M. *Natural History of Love.* London: Hutchinson, 1960.

de ROUGEMONT, Denis. *Passion and Society.* London: Faber and Faber.

LAROUSSE. *New Larousse Encyclopedia of Mythology.* London: Hamlyn, 1959.

LONGFORD, ed. *Oxford Book of Royal Anecdotes.* Oxford University Press, 1991.

LUCIE-SMITH, Edward. *Sexuality in Western Art.* London: Thames and Hudson, 1972.

de la MARE, Walter. *Love.* London: Faber and Faber, 1943.

NAHMAD, Claire. *Garden Spells: The Magic of Herbs, Trees and Flowers.* London: Pavillion, 1992.

Romantic Period Verse. Oxford, 1993.

TABORI, Paul. *Pictorial History of Love.* London: Spring Books, 1966.

TANNER, Heather and Robin. *Woodland Plants.* Robin Garton Ltd, 1981.

TRAIN, J, ed. *Love.* London: Harper Collins, 1993.

VALENCY, Maurice. *In Praise of Love.* London: MacMillan, 1958.

PICTURE CREDITS

The publisher would like to thank the following for their kind permission to reproduce photographs:
5 Woodmansterne Picture Library; *9* Yale Center for British Art, Paul Mellon Collection; *11* C. M. Dixon; *12* Museo Nazionale, Naples/Scala, Florence; *13* Museo Nazionale, Naples/Scala, Florence; *14* Ashmolean Museum, Oxford/Archiv für Kunst und Geschichte, London; *16* Explorer; *19* British Museum, London; *20* British Museum, London; *23* Villa dei Misteri, Pompeii/Scala, Florence; *24* Wurttembergisches Landesmuseum Stuttgart; *26* Charles Potter Kling Fund, Courtesy Museum of Fine Arts, Boston; *29* C. M. Dixon; *31* Victoria and Albert Museum, London; *32* Prado, Madrid/Bridgeman Art Library, London; *33* Staedel Institute, Frankfurt/ Bridgeman Art Library, London; *34* Museo della Collegiata di Sand'Andrea, Empoli/Bridgeman Art Library, London; *36* Museo della Collegiata di Sand'Andrea, Empoli/Bridgeman Art Library, London; *39* Uffizi Gallery/Scala, Florence; *40* Scala, Florence; *42* Woodmansterne Picture Library (Christ Church Library, Oxford); *45* Prado, Madrid/Bridgeman Art Library, London; *46* The Christopher Wood Gallery, London/Bridgeman Art Library, London; *49* Victoria and Albert Museum; *51* Minton Museum, Royal Doulton PLC; *52* Hermitage, St. Petersburg/Bridgeman Art Library, London; *53* Wallace Collection, London/Archiv fur Kunst und Geschichte, London; *54* above, Musée des Tissus, Lyon; *59* Victoria and Albert Museum; *66* Fine Art Photographic; *68* Château de Versailles/Lauros-Giraudon/Bridgeman Art Library, London; *71* Angelo Hornak; *72* Château de Versailles/ Lauros-Giraudon/Bridgeman Art Library, London; *75* The Robert Opie Collection; *76* Laing Art Gallery, Newcastle-upon-Tyne/ Bridgeman Art Library, London; *77* Christie's Images; *79* Uffizi Gallery/Scala, Florence; *82* The Robert Opie Collection; *85* Visual Arts Library; *86* Woodmansterne Picture Library; *88* Retrograph Archive; *90* Musée des Beaux-Arts, Rouen/ Lauros-Giraudon/Bridgeman Art Library, London; *95* 'Heart A' © Paul Giovanopoulos 1989/Courtesy Louis K. Meisel Gallery, New York/Photo: Steve Lopez; *96* Photograph © 1994, The Art Institute of Chicago. All Rights Reserved; *97* Bridgeman Art Library, London/© DACS London 1995; *99* Bridgeman Art Library, London; *101* Museo D'Arte Moderna, Venice/ Bridgeman Art Library, London; *102* Christie's London/Bridgeman Art Library, London/© DACS 1995; *104* John Crook ; *106* Collection L. Treillard/© The Man Ray Trust/ADAGP, Paris and DACS, London 1995; *111* © 1995 Andy Warhol Foundation for the Visual Arts, Inc./ARS, NY and DACS, London 1995; *112* Philadelphia Museum of Art: The Louise and Walter Arensberg Collection/©DACS, London 1995.

QUOTE CREDITS

7 Extract from *The Prophet* by Kahlil Gibran, original publisher William Heinemann Ltd; *96* "sweet spring is your' is reprinted from *Complete Poems 1904–1962*, by E. E. Cummings, edited by George J. Firmage, by permission of W. W. Norton & Company Ltd. Copyright © 1944, 1972, 1991 by the Trustees for the E. E. Cummings Trust; *97* and *99* Extracts from *Gloire de Dijon* and *Young Wife* by D. H. Lawrence, by permission of Laurence Pollinger Ltd and the Estate of Frieda Lawrence Ravagli; *106* ' in spite of everything' is reprinted from *Complete Poems 1904–1962*, by E. E. Cummings, edited by George J. Firmage, by permission of W. W. Norton & Company Ltd. Copyright © 1926, 1954, 1985, 1991 by the Trustees for the E. E. Cummings Trust and George James Firmage; *111* Extract from 'Twelve Songs XII', *W. H. Auden: Collected Poems* by W. H. Auden, copyright © 1940 and renewed 1968 by W. H. Auden. Reprinted by permission of Random House Inc.

INDEX